"I love this book. It's a powerful reminder that one's legacy isn't something left at the end of one's days. It's left every day in little ways. The sum of all those little things is how we're remembered and how we contribute. Jann Freed's *Breadcrumb Legacy* is chock full of meaningful insights, sage advice, provocative questions, and engaging stories. It's also great fun to read... the kind of book where you can turn to any page and find something meaningful and memorable. I highly recommend it to everyone interested in leading a life that makes a difference to self and others."

Jim Kouzes, *coauthor of the bestselling* The Leadership Challenge *and Executive Fellow, Doerr Institute for New Leaders, Rice University*

"You may think you understand the concept of legacy, but Jann Freed's *Breadcrumb Legacy* provides a nuanced approach that you won't find elsewhere. Welcome her as a mentor, teacher, and scholar of this crucial topic."

Bruce Rosenstein, *Managing Editor,* Leader to Leader; *author of* Create Your Future the Peter Drucker Way *and* Living in More Than One World: How Peter Drucker's Wisdom Can Inspire and Transform Your Life

"What on earth are you here for? Few students of leadership and life have thought as long and deeply about this question and the power of living a purposeful life as Jann Freed. Her book offers a perfect blend of wisdom and daily small practices to live a life, ultimately, worth your precious time on earth. It's an inspiring read that could change your life."

Richard Leider, *International bestselling author,* The Power of Purpose, Repacking Your Bags, *and* Who Do You Want to Be When You Grow Old?

"Your legacy is not simply about how you want to be remembered, nor about who you were - it's about who you want to be and what kind of impact you want to have right now. Jann Freed offers a fresh perspective on some of the most important aspects of leadership and your life. I encourage you to read *Breadcrumb Legacy* to align your actions with your good intentions."

Jesse Lyn Stoner, *coauthor* Full Steam Ahead! Unleash the Power of Vision *and* Leading at a Higher Level

"Jann Freed has devoted her life to helping people live with meaning. Her book *Breadcrumb Legacy* can help you leave a trail of daily meaning that will make you proud."

ark Levy, *Founder, Levy Innovation LLC*

T0383046

"We talk a lot about legacy these days, but usually later in life. Jann Freed advocates instead that we think of legacy as the impact we have as a result of daily small actions—breadcrumbs. Adopting this frame can make us better people and more effective leaders. I believe Jann's book will have a long shelf life because it can change how you live your life every day."

Sally Helgesen, *author of* How Women Rise, The Female Advantage, *and* The Web of Inclusion

"My mission is to help successful people achieve positive, lasting behavioral change; for themselves, their people, and their teams. My goal is to help them make their lives a little better! Jann's book, *Breadcrumb Legacy: How Great Leaders Live a Life Worth Remembering*, has really spoken to me as a chance to be thinking about how my positive influence will outlive me. Not only does Jann show readers how 'legacy thinking' can be used as a driving force for daily life, but also how legacy happens in 'crumbs' that accumulate over time. I highly recommend this book and believe in the lasting impact it can have on your life!"

Marshall Goldsmith, *one of the world's leading executive coaches and the* New York Times *bestselling author of* Triggers, Mojo, *and* What Got You Here Won't Get You There

"There are numerous books about leadership and living a quality life. But Jann Freed's *Breadcrumb Legacy: How Great Leaders Live a Life Worth Remembering* integrates these concepts in ways that will help people of all ages live fully and well. She addresses critical topics that are too often ignored: death, relationships, purpose and meaning, the shadow side of the ego. She offers practical exercises to help you live your best life at home and at work. *Breadcrumb Legacy* shows how to leave a legacy by living a life that matters, now and into the future."

Parker J. Palmer, *author of* Let Your Life Speak, The Courage to Teach, *and* On the Brink of Everything

"Leadership in the world of business today isn't just about business: it is about the pursuit of harmony among the different parts of life in a way that brings others along with you toward your vision of a better tomorrow. Jann Freed's *Breadcrumb Legacy* has essential ingredients for realizing this aspiration, at any stage of life. Through research, interviews, and personal stories, Jann shows how to cultivate a meaningful legacy by living a life worth remembering every day."

Stew Friedman, *author of* Total Leadership *and* Professor of Management Practice Emeritus, The Wharton School

"Servant leaders should be thinking about how their words and actions affect others. Leaders who truly serve and empower others live a life worth remembering. Jann's concept of viewing legacy—moment by moment—on a daily basis as a way to guide how we act, say, and do is a great contribution. We live and leave our legacy *now* not later. The sooner we understand this, the better."

Howard Behar, *Former president of Starbucks Coffee Company and author of* It's Not about The Coffee: Leadership Principles from a Life at Starbucks

"Living one's best life is a 'long game' and our actions accumulate. But as Jann Freed shows, building our legacy happens every day. We have the power to choose wisely, live intentionally, and use legacy as our guiding light."

Dorie Clark, Wall Street Journal *Bestselling Author of* The Long Game *and executive education faculty at Duke University's Fuqua School of Business*

"Several years ago, I started my Friday Forward newsletter in the form of a weekly email to my Acceleration Partners team. After reading *Breadcrumb Legacy*, I realize these emails are breadcrumbs—pieces of my leadership legacy I leave each week. *Breadcrumb Legacy* identifies how to raise your game, bring the best out of others, and leave a lasting impact. Everyone wants to make a difference in life, but too many of us wait too long to do it. *Breadcrumb Legacy* reminds us that we can create legacy, in small morsels, every day."

Robert Glazer, *author of* Elevate *and Founder and Board Chairman of Acceleration Partners*

"You often hear celebrities, when interviewed by journalists, asked the question 'How do you want to be remembered?' This isn't just a question for celebrities. All of us should think about it. We will be remembered if we act each day as if our choices matter. Jann shares how to act thoughtfully, breadcrumb by breadcrumb, and live a life with remembering."

Suzanne Bates, *author of* All the Leader You Can Be: The Science of Achieving Extraordinary Executive Presence

"If you have ever wondered about what people will think of you when you are out of their lives, you are thinking the 'L' word: legacy. *Breadcrumb Legacy* is a terrific resource for determining how to think about, plan, and live a life that will be remembered—not because you were great, but because you helped those around you live better lives. Packed with stories and interviews, *Breadcrumb Legacy* will make you think about how you can make a positive difference."

John Baldoni, *author of* Grace Notes: Leading in an
Upside-Down World

"As I always say to my executive coaching clients, as well as to the students in my NYU and Columbia leadership graduate courses: Think about what you would want people to say about you at your 'retirement party'…and then determine what it is that you will actually need to do between now and then to make that vision a reality. Towards this end, in her wonderful new book, *Breadcrumb Legacy*, leadership expert Jann Freed turns that mission into a metaphor of mindset, meaning, and moments that will inspire us to live our best lives and become our best selves…while leaving behind a trail of wisdom and inspiration for others to follow."

Todd Cherches, *CEO of BigBlueGumball and author
of* VisuaLeadership: Leveraging the Power of Visual
Thinking in Leadership and in Life

"Many people think about legacy toward the end of their career or the end of life. 'Dr. Jann' Freed challenges us to think differently. No matter what age you are, she advocates thinking of legacy daily as your North Star—a compass to guide your thoughts and actions to stay on your right path. Filled with her own stories and supplemented by insights from a variety of leaders, *Breadcrumb Legacy* provides a roadmap for integrating leading with living. Be sure to sample Dr. Jann's 'breadcrumb ingredients,' exercises and practical tips on applying the chapter concepts. These can help you along the journey for becoming the best version of yourself at work and in every other aspect of life."

Pamela S. Harper, *Founding Partner & CEO of
Business Advancement Inc., author of* Preventing Strategic
Gridlock, *and co-host of* Growth Igniters® Radio

"It is easy to forget that everywhere we go, others are experiencing us. It's only when we remember how we show up matters, that we can be more intentional about what we say, what we do, and how we act. Jann Freed's concept of *Breadcrumb Legacy* reminds us that we are leaving 'crumbs' every day that make an impression—good or bad. *Breadcrumb Legacy* is about showing up and being present so that you are living in the way you want to be remembered, and doing this day after day, which accumulates into a life well lived."

Rob Salafia, *author of* Leading From Your Best
Self: Develop Executive Poise, Presence, and
Influence to Maximize Your Potential

"Leaving a legacy is the great task of later life, and *Breadcrumb Legacy: How Great Leaders Live a Life Worth Remembering* is a timeless testament to what must be done. While other books talk about legacy, Jann shows us *how* to live a life in the way you want to be remembered."

Harry "Rick" Moody, retired Vice President for Academic Affairs, AARP

"*Breadcrumb Legacy* is a guidebook for old souls who want to make a difference every day of their lives. Jann's inspiring message is that building a legacy is a developmental task and it's never too early (or late) to begin. This is a must-have for the conscious aging library and a wonderful addition to the impressive body of literature coming out of the Sage-ing movement."

Carol Orsborn, PhD, *author of* The Making of an Old Soul *and* Older, Wiser, Fiercer

"Jann Freed knows that what you choose to do is important, but she knows also that how you choose to be is even more important. And she knows that the small everyday things you choose to do will define, to a great extent, how you choose to be, because those everyday actions which she calls 'breadcrumbs' become the evidence of your character and the legacy of your leadership, day after day. We need this message now more than ever. Bravo, Jann!"

James A. Autry, *author of* The Servant Leader: How To Build A Creative Team, Develop Great Morale, and Improve Bottom-Line Performance

"Today's world is aching for greater meaning and impact. But too many of us wait too long before we realize we don't have enough. In *Breadcrumb Legacy,* Jann Freed wisely advocates for the small steps we can each take every day to amass a significant impact on the world around us. If you want to ensure your indelible fingerprint is left on the world in ways you'd be proud to have others emulate, read this book slowly."

Ron Carucci, *Managing Partner at Navalent author of* To Be Honest *and* Rising to Power

"We don't achieve immortality by acquiring things for ourselves. Rather, we achieve immortality by using our time and talents to help others grow. Our legacy is found in the breadcrumbs. The little notes of love we put in our kid's lunchbox. The hot coffee we give to a homeless man. Jann Freed's superb book *Breadcrumb Legacy* is a gift to anyone who's ready to craft a life worth remembering."

John P. Weiss, *author of* An Artful Life: Inspirational Stories and Essays for the Artist in Everyone

"Legacy, and writing legacy letters, had been the focus of my work for the last 25 years, when I took on the mission of giving women their voices in writing. *Breadcrumb Legacy* includes legacy letters and more. Jann sees life through a legacy perspective and you will find legacy values on every page of her inspirational and down to earth new book. Jann stands on the shoulders of those who renewed interest in legacy in the last century. Her focus on leadership and 'breadcrumbs' takes legacy literature to a new level. Jann's book has both legacy concepts, the bread, and exercises and tips, breadcrumbs, to bring the concepts to daily life. I recommend her book to all adults, young people and elders."

Rachael A. Freed, LICSW, LMFT, *founder of Life-Legacies and author of* Heartmates, A Guide for the Partner and Family of the Heart Patient; Women's Lives, Women's Legacies: Passing Your Beliefs and Blessings to Future Generations; The Legacy Workbook for the Busy Woman; *and* Your Legacy Matters

"Jann is a powerful ally and leader in my quest to enable people to make the second half of life their best, their most meaningful and their most impactful. What *Breadcrumb Legacy: How Great Leaders Live a Life Worth Remembering* provides is the practical and aspirational methods and mindsets to embrace to leave a meaningful legacy, and to enjoy the most relevant and purposeful years of one's life. This book should be required reading for all stages of life because each stage is a gift."

Paul Long, *Founder New Way Forward*

"Leaving a personal legacy has become top of mind for people of all ages, as we all have faced mortality over the last several years. Jann Freed has developed a bold new approach to your legacy that will serve as a compass as we seek our True North."

Bill George, *author of* True North, Emerging Leader Edition, *Executive Fellow, Harvard Business School and former CEO, Medtronic*

Breadcrumb Legacy

Legacy can seem far off and out of reach, but it doesn't happen at journey's end and it's not only for the rich and famous. Legacy is now, and this book shows leaders how you can find and leave meaning on a daily basis. Jann E. Freed, PhD, introduces her Breadcrumb Legacy™ framework, a radical but pragmatic approach, made up of small actions you consciously take over time that accumulate into the trail, or legacy, you'll leave behind.

Breadcrumb Legacy is also a mindset, an awareness of the impact you're having on your relationships, your organization, and your family, in every communication and interaction.

This book is the guide to leaving a trail of meaning throughout your life and career. Based on in-depth interviews, *Breadcrumb Legacy* provides inspiration and practical stories for living a life worth remembering.

Jann E. Freed, PhD, is Professor of Business Management Emerita at Central College and the Mark and Kay De Cook Endowed Chair in Leadership and Character Development.

She is also an adjunct professor for the University of Iowa.

As a leadership development coach, consultant, author, facilitator, and speaker, Jann helps organizations improve employee engagement, navigate change management, and develop leaders of all ages and career stages.

She has written or co-written five books, given two popular TEDx talks, and is a Certified Sage-ing Leader through Sage-ing International. Jann also hosts the podcast series *Becoming a Sage*, where she interviews thought leaders about wisdom in work and in life.

Jann's personal mission is to continue to learn and share what she's learning with others. As a wisdom seeker, she often says that she likes teaching, but is passionate about learning. This book has changed her life.

Breadcrumb Legacy

How Great Leaders Live a Life Worth Remembering

Jann E. Freed, PhD

Routledge
Taylor & Francis Group

NEW YORK AND LONDON

Designed cover image: Ron Barrett and Valerie Kennedy

First published 2023
by Routledge
605 Third Avenue, New York, NY 10158

and by Routledge
4 Park Square, Milton Park, Abingdon, Oxon, OX14 4RN

Routledge is an imprint of the Taylor & Francis Group, an informa business

Library of Congress Cataloging-in-Publication Data
Names: Freed, Jann E., author.
Title: Breadcrumb legacy : how great leaders live a life worth remembering / Jann E. Freed. Description: New York, NY : Routledge, 2023. | Includes bibliographical references and index. Identifiers: LCCN 2022027651 (print) | LCCN 2022027652 (ebook) | ISBN 9781032315447 (hardback) | ISBN 9781032315430 (paperback) | ISBN 9781003310211 (ebook) Subjects: LCSH: Values. | Creative ability. | Motivation (Psychology) | Quality of life. | Leadership. Classification: LCC BF778 .F69 2023 (print) | LCC BF778 (ebook) | DDC 158—dc23/eng/20220914 LC record available at https://lccn.loc.gov/2022027651 LC ebook record available at https://lccn.loc.gov/2022027652

ISBN: 9781032315447 (hbk)
ISBN: 9781032315430 (pbk)
ISBN: 9781003310211 (ebk)

DOI: 10.4324/9781003310211

Typeset in Bembo
by codeMantra

In Memory

I met Dr. Elmer Burack, a former professor at the University of Illinois at Chicago, at the Midwest Business Administration Association International (MBAAI). Elmer was the discussant for my paper and asked if he could give me additional feedback after my session.

Elmer told me he had found a source missing in my bibliography. The source was cited in the paper, but the complete citation was not in the list of references. I knew it was missing, but this was years before the Internet, and I could not find it after hours of looking. From my numerous years of experience at this conference, I knew most reviewers did not read papers that carefully. Based on our short conversation, I knew I could learn a lot from Elmer.

So right then and there I invited Elmer to lunch and thus began a 20-year mentorship and friendship. He set me on the path of Sage-ing©. Sage-ing International defines Sage-ing as "aging consciously through life's transitions and challenges in community with like-minded older adults." The world lost Elmer's wisdom in 2012 and his 82 years of life experience.

But Elmer's legacy lives on in me. What I learned from him, I have passed on to thousands of students and continue to share in my work. I still ask myself, "What would Elmer do?"

Contents

Author Biography

About the Author: Jann E. Freed, PhD

As a leadership development coach, consultant, and speaker, organizations hire me to improve employee engagement, navigate change management, and develop leaders of all ages and career stages. But I am a wisdom seeker who has always respected and admired my elders.

I am the author or co-author of five books. For my most recent book, *Leading with Wisdom: Sage Advice from 100 Experts,* I interviewed prominent leadership gurus such as Jim Autry, Peter Block, Marshall Goldsmith, Sally Helgesen, and Margaret Wheatley.

I am Professor of Business Management Emerita at Central College, Pella, Iowa, where I held the Mark and Kay De Cook Endowed Chair in Leadership and Character Development. Since leaving Central, I have been an adjunct professor for the University of Iowa teaching a graduate leadership course.

In addition to college teaching, I've conducted workshops for more than 30 years. I share what I am learning through speaking, coaching, teaching, and writing. I have a column titled 'Leading Edge' in *Training Magazine*—in each print and online issue.

Community involvement is a priority. It is important for me to practice what I am teaching and learning along the way.

In 2007, I became certified as a Sage-ing Leader through Sage-ing International. On my website, I blog and write a newsletter about learning, leading, living, and Sage-ing. For several years, I have hosted a podcast series, *Becoming a Sage,* where I interview top thought leaders to seek wisdom about leading and living with purpose and meaning.

I've been selected twice as a TEDx speaker. For TEDxDesMoines, my talk *Embracing Death: Seeing Life through a Different Lens* explains one component of my Breadcrumb Manifesto: that we can embrace life more easily if we confront death head-on. For my TEDxBergenCommunityCollege talk *Becoming a Nobody*, I discussed how controlling the ego can help us become better leaders and better people.

Foreword

Don't you love it when you meet someone who feels like a long-lost friend? Someone who could finish your sentences for you? That's been my relationship with your author, Jann.

After I wrote my last book, *Wisdom@Work: The Making of a Modern Elder*, Jann reached out to interview me for her podcast series titled *Becoming a Sage*. The first time the Modern Elder Academy (MEA) offered an online course, Jann was one of the first people to sign up. She has even written a guest post for my blog *Wisdom Well*. Given what I know about Jann, I would say we are connected because of our love of concepts such as wisdom, curiosity, and creativity.

Our paths are somewhat parallel because we are both interested in helping people live their best lives. I am doing that through founding the Modern Elder Academy in Baja, California Sur, Mexico, and Santa Fe, New Mexico. We now have more than 1,500 alumni from 28 countries. Jann shares her knowledge through writing, teaching, and coaching.

Many of the people Jann interviews for this book, *Breadcrumb Legacy: How Great Leaders Live a Life Worth Remembering*, and her podcast are guest faculty at MEA. Her resources are some of the same ones we draw upon— Richard Leider, Barbara Waxman, Bruce Feiler, William Bridges, and Parker Palmer. There is no doubt Jann is a student of leading and living. The way she integrates these concepts is unique and valuable.

We call MEA a "midlife wisdom school" and it is often misunderstood to be purely for elders. But midlife happens earlier than we often think. If the average life expectancy is about 80, then 40 is midlife and 49 the precise center of adulthood (spanning from 18 to 80). So, this is a ripe time to imagine how we want to spend the second half of our adult lives.

When should you think about your legacy? Most people wait until late in life and often think their legacy has to be some big and monumental task or building. People often associate legacy with money and philanthropy. But Breadcrumb Legacy™ is the opposite. It is thinking about legacy daily as a way to stay on the right path. If you think about how you want to be remembered, then you can use that vision to make decisions and take actions that are congruent. As Jann likes to say, "the earlier someone understands these concepts, the better."

In this book, Jann not only explains the concepts but she describes *how* to leave a path of which you will be proud. Jann has clearly joined the movement of making the rest of life the best of life her mantra. Her Breadcrumb Legacy Manifesto includes six components of which the book is organized:

Having a purpose
Having a growth mindset
Cultivating, nurturing, and sustaining relationships
Embracing death
Becoming a nobody
Sharing wisdom

Each of these components could be a workshop and more at MEA. Jann's work complements all of what I believe about consciously living. This book can be a roadmap for living a positive life worth remembering.

Chip Conley
New York Times Bestselling Author and Founder
of Modern Elder Academy

Acknowledgments

As I reflected on everyone I want to thank for helping my passion become a reality, the metaphor that came to mind was of me following a journey of breadcrumbs for the last several years. Where do the crumbs begin?

As my professional mentor, Dr. Elmer Burack mailed me the classic book by Zalman Schachter-Shalomi *From Aging to Sage-ing: A Revolutionary Approach to Growing Older.* Elmer encouraged me to become certified as a Sage-ing Leader through Sage-ing© International. He strongly believed that with people living longer they were going to need some guidance and that could be my calling. Anything Elmer suggested I do, I did. His crumbs started the journey.

All that I learned through my involvement in Sage-ing International informed the research for my first book, *Leading with Wisdom: Sage Advice from 100 Experts.* One of the topics that resonated the most with me was how leaders live their legacy, so the book integrates the daily practice of leadership with everyday living.

Then I was listening to a podcast with Samantha Slade, author of *Going Horizontal: Creating a Non-Hierarchical Organization, One Practice at a Time.* During the interview, Slade mentions she would not have written this book without her writing coach. I immediately sent her a tweet and asked if she would share the name and contact information of her coach. A day later, she tweeted: "Mark Levy of Levy Innovation." A crumb.

Within days, I had a conversation with Mark. I decided to work with him to come up with my big, sexy idea for my book. During the months I worked with Mark, it became clear I needed to increase my online presence. He suggested I contact a woman he had met at a conference who was a social media expert named Marie Incontrera. Another crumb.

I hired Marie to enhance my personal brand on social media, which she did. As a result of working with Marie, I had two TEDx talks in 2021—each on a different chapter in this book. Then Marie encouraged me to check out Dorie Clark's Recognized Expert™ course. After listening to one webinar with Dorie, I joined her REx community and have not looked back. Again, another crumb.

I continue to learn and meet new people in the REx community. One of the members I met early on was Pam Harper, CEO of Business Advancement, Inc. Pam, author of *Preventing Strategic Gridlock: Leading Over, Under, & Around Organizational Jams to Achieve High Performance Results,* led me to contact her literary agent Ken Lizotte. Ken is the Chief Imaginative Officer and founder of emerson consulting group. A crumb I followed.

As I was shopping around for publishers, Ken said to me, "Give me a shot at this book!" So I did. Ken assigned me his daughter, Chloe Lizotte, as my editor. Chloe was the perfect editor for me. She is an excellent writer, educated at Yale, and her youth was an asset. Since I wanted to write this book for an audience with a wide age range, Chloe prevented me from becoming too focused on the second half of life.

While I was working on this book, I continued to be involved in Sageing International (SI) and I discovered Chip Conley's book *Wisdom@ Work.* Chip's book was the stimulus for his founding the Modern Elder Academy (MEA) in Baja, California, and a forthcoming campus in Santa Fe, New Mexico.

Chip and I are both seekers of wisdom, and he has informed my work in many ways. He allowed me to interview him for my podcast, *Becoming a Sage.* His daily blog titled *Wisdom Well* scatters daily crumbs; I pick them up to start my day. In July of 2022, I spent two weeks at the campus in Baja. The first week I attended a workshop and the second week was a personal sabbatical—MEA SabSesh.

I continue to follow the crumbs in front of me. Being an active member of REx, SI, and MEA has enabled me to interview a variety of corporate and thought leaders who would have been challenging to contact—or even impossible. Thank you to all of my interviewees who shared their crumbs of wisdom with me.

More crumbs led to the final book cover. Since my son MacLean (Mac) is in the marketing field, I sent the draft cover to him for feedback. Jessica Barrett, my daughter-in-law, forwarded the draft cover to her father, Ron Barrett, who is a professional illustrator. With the creative insight of Ron and Valerie Kennedy, the cover was created with actual breadcrumbs and Ron's special bird.

My journey would not be complete if I did not thank my students over the years, both undergraduate and graduate. Since starting this research in 2007, I have shared what I have been learning with students and they have been receptive. My main message is that your legacy is *now*: regardless of your age or stage in life. And the sooner we all realize this, the better.

Finally, I'd like to thank one of the main "crumbs" in my life—my husband, John Fisher. He has supported my research and allowed me the freedom to follow my dreams and passion to Baja and beyond. John and my three sons—MacLean (Mac), Austin, and Marshall—have listened to me talk endlessly about the topics in this book. Some of the resources I cite in this book were crumbs they shared with me with notes such as *Thought you'd enjoy this! This is a story you will love! You should interview this person! This person is a Sage for sure.*

Everything I see, read, listen to, or watch seems to relate to some aspect of legacy. This work has changed my life. Nike said it best: There is no finish line. My editor and publisher said that the book had to end. But the Breadcrumb Legacy journey will never end.

To everyone who has influenced me through their crumbs, please know that I am grateful.

Chapter 1

What Breadcrumbs Are You Leaving Behind?

Should I look at the letters on top of my son's desk or not?

I decided to look.

A month earlier, Mac had graduated from college and moved to New York City for a job. At the time, he had a college girlfriend and on top of his desk was a bundle of cards and notes. I assumed the letters were from her.

I would pass by his room and my curiosity was getting the best of me. One day, I couldn't help but take a quick peek at the top of his desk. Well, I thought, Mac left them there and he was out of sight.

All of the notes and cards were from me over the years, from when he was a ten-year-old at camp all the way through college. He even kept notes that were not positive. There were cards I wrote to him about being disappointed in his behavior in middle school.

Mac is the oldest and has younger twin brothers. I had a unique practice for teaching all of them how to learn from their mistakes. When they did something that required discipline, I would have them write a letter to me explaining what they had done wrong, why they had done it, and why they wouldn't do it again. Some of these notes were still on his desk.

When I realized that Mac had held onto everything I had written to him over the years, I started my long-standing tradition of writing each of them legacy letters on their birthdays.

These letters have become significant breadcrumbs for me over the years.

What Makes a Legacy?

Habit number two in Stephen Covey's *The Seven Habits of Highly Effective People* is "Begin with the end in mind."

I often ask leaders to tell me when we leave our legacy. Most of them say:

When we retire.
When we die.
When we leave a job.
When we leave.

DOI: 10.4324/9781003310211-1

"Leave what?" I ask in return. "What about when I leave this room? Leave a meeting? Leave a conversation or interaction?"

Leaving happens in so many different ways every day. We leave relationships. Locations. Religious and political affiliations.

In truth, we leave our legacy as breadcrumbs all of the time. Your legacy can guide your daily behaviors—big and small. If we start with the end in mind, we think about what we can do every day to reach our desired end.

I once asked Connie Wimer, chairperson of *Business Publications*, about defining moments in her leadership journey. "There have not been any real defining moments," she told me, "but there have been a million baby steps."

Breadcrumbs.

Legacy with a Little "L"

The word "legacy" usually comes up when someone dies. The word is also associated with professional athletes and celebrities, since they tend to retire earlier as they "age out" of their profession. For years, people have wondered when Roger Federer or Warren Buffett might retire, and journalists talk about the legacy they are leaving.

The problem with this perception, though, is that it encourages us to think of greatness and achievements that are extraordinary. Any goals to attain this kind of legacy seem out of reach for most of us.

Merriam-Webster defines legacy as "a gift by will, especially of money or other personal property" or "something transmitted by or received from an ancestor or predecessor or from the past." Although we might think of legacy as an inheritance at the end of life, there is so much more we leave behind. Whether it's positive or negative, every day we are making an impression that people remember.

Breadcrumb Legacy presents a new vision for legacy. It is based on understanding the everyday impact of our actions, decisions, and behaviors. When leaders are conscious of even their smallest actions, they reflect more deeply on the difference they are making. It is about being consciously intentional about what we say and do. This framework, and even this mindset, comprises *Breadcrumb Legacy*.

This concept isn't only for just the rich and famous, or simply for CEOs and senior leaders. *Breadcrumb Legacy* can make a difference for all people who are in a position to influence the lives of others. This definition includes parents, coaches, teachers, pastors, and others.

In other words, *Breadcrumb Legacy* is designed for everyone who wants to live a life of daily meaning. The idea is summed up in this quote from Studs Terkel, the Pulitzer Prize–winning author of *Working: People Talk About What They Do All Day and How They Feel About What They Do*:

Work is about a search for daily meaning as well as daily bread, for recognition as well as cash, for astonishment rather than torpor; in short, for a sort of life rather than a Monday through Friday sort of dying.

Or, consider how Suzanne Bates, author of *All the Leader You Can Be*, described her outlook during our interview: "You are creating your legacy every day. As you grow and change, your legacy grows too. We leave our imprint everywhere. We should be conscious of the legacy we are leaving both large and small."

In a given day, there are practically unlimited opportunities to create—and seize—legacy moments. For example, Robert Glazer, the founder and CEO of Acceleration Partners, writes an inspirational email to all of his employees every Friday. His main focus is elevating performance in both business and life.

In fact, Glazer compiled these Friday emails into his book *Friday Forward: Inspiration & Motivation to End Your Week Stronger Than It Started*. As I read his book and reviewed his top ten posts for the year, I discovered that most of his posts related to legacy.

Glazer told me he was awakened to the idea of legacy when he was asked to write his eulogy in a leadership development course (more on this type of exercise to come in Chapter 5). The experience taught him that he wanted others to become better people simply for having known him.

He characterized breadcrumbs as personal touches that are unexpected. "No one really thanks you for bonuses because they earned it and expect it," he observed. "So I send gifts out of the blue to team members to show appreciation for their work, and they remember it."

In many cases, these unprompted moments will instill our values in others. Rachael Freed, founder of Life-Legacies and a Senior Fellow at the University of Minnesota's Center for Spirituality and Healing (no relationship, but I wish), explained to me how she started a reading group with her grandchildren over Zoom during the COVID-19 pandemic.

"By doing this, I am communicating my relationship with reading and the importance of reading," Freed reflected. "Our whole life is a legacy... it is what others observe and perceive."

Likewise, Tim Hebert, CEO of Trilix told me, "Legacy moments are those things you don't have to do—no one is forcing you to do them. When we don't expect them, others remember them. Even smiling can be a legacy moment."

Some of the crumbs that have been meaningful to me I kept in a particular desk drawer: special notes from decades of students, words of wisdom that are "gems" to remember, random acts of kindness, a friend apologizing for hurting my feelings.

Since so many people rely on email for communication, I like to leave handwritten notes as breadcrumbs. Often, I write them on postcards I create myself, either from my own photographs or featuring my favorite quotes. I send these postcards as thank-you notes and I distribute them in my workshops and classes. Scattering my breadcrumbs as part of my life.

We think "legacy" has to be written with a "BIG L" when it's really a "little l." What we are talking about are the little things that make a big difference.

Breadcrumb Box:

A few years ago, I took a faith-based social justice course. For one of the final assignments, we had to select a project that put what we learned to practice.

In an earlier session, we talked about the practice of handing out money to homeless people: What if they use it for cigarettes or drugs? Pope Francis was once asked this very question. He responded that the money given is a gift. Rather than focus on what you are giving, what matters most is that you look the other person in the eye. Acknowledge that they matter.

So, for this assignment, I created what I now call Breadcrumb Bags. I fill a quart-sized Ziploc bag with practical, but small items that might have a big impact for people who stand at street corners. Included are travel size hand sanitizer, toothbrush and paste, granola bars, socks, and a few dollars.

I always look the other person in the eye and say something to them. The only downside is I am clogging up traffic, but that doesn't matter to me.

This has been my practice ever since. In fact, I blogged about it and several people told me they are following my lead and making their own Breadcrumb Bags.

A Million Tiny Little Things

It is important to realize that our breadcrumbs may not always be positive. If we aren't careful, we could leave a trail that we may not be proud of at the end of life.

In my PhD program, there was a professor I will call "Dr. Smith." He taught a quantitative course and was feared by all students. His style was similar to Professor Kingsfield in the classic movie *The Paper Chase*. Like Professor Kingsfield, Dr. Smith was stern, never smiled, and used the Socratic method of randomly calling on people.

It was common knowledge that students felt Dr. Smith prided himself on scaring us by putting us on the spot and actually humiliating us in front of the class. Even though I concluded his bark was worse than his bite, his reputation preceded him and followed him after he retired.

Several years later, I asked one of Dr. Smith's colleagues what had happened to him. She mentioned that he had passed away. I remarked how we all dreaded his courses because of his style of using fear to motivate.

She proceeded to tell me about his funeral. The family gave strict instructions to attendees: "No one is allowed to speak unless previously approved." She said they were afraid of what some people might say about him.

What a sad ending, I thought to myself. What a legacy he left for others to remember.

Breadcrumb Box:

Jim Kouzes, co-author of *The Leadership Challenge* and Fellow at Rice University's Doerr Institute for New Leaders, shared this story in our interview:

> My wife and I were in a small town in California at the base of Lake Tahoe. We walked into this old railroad building that had been renovated into a store. On the side of the building was a carved wooden sign:
>
> "This building is dedicated to the memory of Ignatious Joseph Furpo. What we have done for ourselves dies with us. What we have done for others remains and is immortal."
>
> When I talk about legacy, this is one of the first slides I show. It is a reminder to me and my wife of what people remember about us. Our legacy includes the stories people tell about us after we are gone. How would you like to be talked about when you are no longer around (the organization)? What lessons did they learn from you? How did people feel about you? What is the tangible evidence that you made a difference?
>
> The old Boy Scout in me remembers: Leave the campsite better than you found it.

Creating a Path

A lot is written about "the second half of life," which arrives sooner than we think. If the average life expectancy is 80, then 40 is the midpoint. And these days, we are healthier and living longer than past generations. Joseph Coughlin, director of the Massachusetts Institute of Technology AgeLab, says we may live an additional 30 years after retirement or 8,000 days.

How will you make the most of these 8,000 days?

You are living your legacy right now. But are you living the way you want to be remembered?

When we are aware of the breadcrumbs we are leaving, we are engaged in *legacy thinking,* which is actually *forward-thinking.* When people, especially those in leadership roles, reflect on how their actions, decisions, and behaviors will impact others, they should be more intentional about what they say, the decisions they make, and how they behave.

With our awakening to legacy thinking, we walk into uncharted territory. *Breadcrumb Legacy* can help us make a path—to know the way—as we intentionally leave breadcrumbs for others to follow. Our legacy will live on through these crumbs, which means that what's important to us won't be lost.

For Ron Carucci, author of *To Be Honest: Lead with the Power of Truth, Justice, and Purpose,* legacy is a verb. "I'm going to legacy today—legacy moments," he declared. Yet, he also told me how often he hears the word "legacy" used in conversations about regrets, or unfinished business.

"In life there is no 'do over,'" he pointed out. "So we need to make sure our fingerprint is one of which we are proud."

This isn't a consideration exclusive to leaders in the second half of life, either—the earlier we focus on it, the better. "It is never too early to start thinking about legacy because it is cumulative," Carucci continued. "It is hard to uncreate it or reverse engineer it unless we intentionally work at that ... The trail we are leaving behind becomes the 'picture' of our life."

When I interviewed Georgia-based "coachsultant" Peter Chatel, he also described legacy as something that's generative. "Legacy is about your life story. We are fortunate because we can grow and change if we are intentional," he noted. "How might you reframe your story? Instead of living with regret or shame, we can do something about it before it is too late—if we are awake and aware."

Most of us want to know that our lives have made a difference. When we create a trail of meaning, no matter how "small" it may seem, every day, it adds up to a legacy: a roadmap of how we want to be remembered.

Mattering matters.

Breadcrumb Box:

Breadcrumbs may not announce themselves as such in the moment. Tim Hebert, CEO of Trilix, shared this story to illustrate a breadcrumb moment.

I was invited to speak at a NFP called Young Voices, which teaches public speaking strategies to inner city high school students.

Before my speech, I was assigned a guide, "John," to give me a tour of the building. I asked him what he wanted to accomplish in life, and his goals were all materialistic. At the end of the day, I said to John, "Everything you've mentioned is about what you can accumulate and acquire. While that is good, life is more than that. It is about how you impact the people around you. That is how you determine wealth."

John graduated, went to college, and then business school. I hadn't talked to him for 5–6 years. The woman who ran Young Voices reached out to me and said John wanted to talk to me. "He wants to thank you."

"Thank me for what?" I responded.

"You had a conversation with him years ago and it changed his life. You made him think about his life in a different way."

I had forgotten the conversation after it happened. But for him, it was a defining moment—you can call it a breadcrumb. I took the time to show an interest in this young man and gave him some advice. He was able to reflect upon it and he made changes going forward.

As we interact with the people around us, we can have a profound impact on them—both in good and in bad ways. We should be intentional about how we interact to make sure that impact is positive. My focus was not on myself and my topic, but to help these kids who have a disadvantage in life, who were born in the wrong zip code.

In that moment, it was all about John. Leaders can get lost in their own dreams and pursuits, but our words, our presence, the way we interact—all matter more than we might imagine. Often, we will never know.

But What Is Meant by Meaning?

In his book *When All You've Ever Wanted Isn't Enough*, Rabbi Harold Kushner shares the story of one of his parishioners, who attended a funeral of one of his peers for the first time. The parishioner was thinking about his own life. He said that the circle of life and death is "like a rock falling into a pool of water. For a few seconds, it makes ripples in the water, and then the water is the same as it was before, but the rock isn't there anymore."

This funeral got his attention. The parishioner resonated with the rock and felt as if his life might not matter.

We want to know at the end of life that our life mattered—that we had a positive impact on the world. Several studies reflect that meaning is often missing in our lives, especially millennials. In a study by the Gallup

Organization, "What Millennials Want from Work and Life," young employees seek organizations with a clear purpose and opportunities to grow. It is easy to chase fame, fortune, and high achievement, thinking it leads to the good life. But younger employees are interested in companies that are making a difference as much as their paycheck and personal performance.

Pick up a self-help book and they all tend to agree that our souls are hungry for meaning, for a sense that the world is a little bit of a better place because we were here. But they usually don't tell you *how* to find that meaning or *how* to practice it daily. Chapter 2 delves into these ideas in greater detail.

"What you do every day matters more than what you do once in a while," advised Gretchen Rubin, author of *The Happiness Project*. Whether that's writing a heartfelt note to family or friends, or remembering to smile at a co-worker, keep in mind that even our smallest breadcrumbs will accumulate into a trail.

Man's Search for Meaning by Holocaust survivor Viktor Frankl is a mainstay on leadership reading lists. For Frankl, one essential component of human purpose is the freedom "to choose one's own way." This consists of two key actions: making decisions about what you *want* to happen, and choosing how you respond to what *does* happen.

When I spoke with David L. Bradford, the Eugene O'Kelly II Senior Lecturer Emeritus in Leadership at Stanford, he linked these concepts back to ripples:

> All of the interactions we have—both large and small—are like when you drop a pebble in a pond. These ripples are part of my legacy, representing all of the people I have influenced—even the unintended consequences in relationships.

Breadcrumb Legacy is about choosing your own way so that you make your life worth remembering—even while you're here, to the people who matter the most.

Breadcrumb Box:

According to Bill George, former CEO of Medtronics and author of *True North*:

> The only real legacy you leave is the people you touched. It is not what was written in the media or a nice obituary. The individuals you touched may be your own family members or the people you worked with whether they were first line people or your leadership team. Were you kind, compassionate, and concerned about them when they were ill or their spouse was ill? Did you reach out to them? It's this kind of humanity that matters most.

> As leaders, people won't remember you for the numbers when you were running the business. They are going to remember who you were as a person. Ages 60–90 are a time of generativity when you can give back to other people.

Breadcrumb Ingredients for Leaving (and Living) a Legacy

Begin with the End in Mind:

You are already leaving a trail behind. Ask yourself these questions to be more intentional about your tracks:

1 Who do you want to grow into? How is your "doing" a reflection of your "being"? Remember you are a human *being*, not a human *doing*.
2 What do you wish you'd known ten years ago that you know now? What can you start learning today that will serve you ten years from now? How can you pass on what you have learned?
3 If you only had five years left to live, how would you alter your current way of living?

Write a Letter to Your Younger Self:

Consider how you have lived your life up until now. Then answer these statements:

My life was well lived because…
My life would've been better if I had done…
I am now going to live my life differently by…

Bibliography

Adkins, A. (2016). "What millennials want from work and life." *Gallup Organization.* https://www.gallup.com/workplace/236477/millennials-work-life.aspx

Bates, S. & Macaux, W. (2016). *All the leader you can be: The science of achieving extraordinary executive presence.* New York: McGraw-Hill.

Carucci, R. (2021). *To be honest: Lead with the power of truth, justice, and purpose.* London: Kogan Books.

Coughlin, J. (April 13, 2019). "Why 8,000 is the most important number for your retirement plan." *Forbes.* https://www.forbes.com/sites/josephcoughlin/2019/04/13/why-8000-is-the-most-important-number-for-your-retirement-plan/?sh=5627dfe042ae

Covey, S. R. (2020). *The 7 habits of highly effective people: Powerful lessons in personal change.* New York: Simon & Schuster.

Frankl, V. E. (2006). *Man's search for meaning.* Boston, MA: Beacon Press.

George, B. & Sims, P. (2007). *True north*. San Francisco, CA: Jossey-Bass.

Glazer, R. (2021). *Friday forward: Inspiration & motivation to end your week stronger than it started*. Naperville, IL: Simple Truths.

Kushner, H. (2002). *When all you've ever wanted isn't enough*. New York: Simon & Schuster.

legacy. (2021). In Merriam-Webster.com. Retrieved September 13, 2021, from https://www.merriam-webster.com/dictionary/legacy

Rubin, G. (2012). *The happiness project*. New York: HarperCollins Publishers.

Terkel, S. (1997). *Working: People talk about what they do all day and how they feel about what they do*. New York: New York Press.

Chapter 2

Why Get Up in the Morning?

When the movie *About Schmidt* came out in 2002, our neighbor Gene told us we must go see it. Gene is a Jack Nicholson impersonator, often portraying him at parties. He was also Nicholson's body double for the movie. Since Gene is a funny guy, we knew the movie would be a comedy.

We were wrong.

The movie, directed by Alexander Payne, follows Warren Schmidt (Nicholson) on his journey of redefining his purpose. In the beginning, Schmidt is unprepared for and depressed by his life after retirement: his career defined him, and his life was his work. Now he has lost his identity: his reason for getting up in the morning.

Then Schmidt's wife dies suddenly. He spirals downward even further. So, he buys an RV and drives around the country, trying to find something new to do with his life, but remains totally clueless as to where he is going and what he will do when he arrives.

After the lights came up, my husband and I looked at each other and asked, "Did you find the movie funny?" We agreed that the movie was unexpectedly sad, but we couldn't stop thinking about it or talking about it.

As we thought about it, I wondered, "If you are what you do and you don't do it anymore, then who are you?"

The Value of Purpose

People get hung up on "work." When we are working, we dream about not working. When we are not working, we can feel lost. Without meaning, purpose, and a sense of legacy, we may survive, but we won't thrive. We are more likely to be disengaged and directionless just like Warren Schmidt.

When you "retire" and leave a career, it is easy to drift without a work identity. It is easy to confuse *what we do* with *who we are*. Moreover, recent trends on divorce, loneliness, depression, suicide, alcohol and drug abuse indicate that people are aimlessly drifting. These data points are alarming, indicating that too many people feel lost at sea.

DOI: 10.4324/9781003310211-2

These feelings aren't limited to retirement: Millennials are known as the Purpose Generation because they want work to be more than a paycheck. In fact, the COVID-19 pandemic gave people time and space to reevaluate their lives. It was time to hit the reset button.

The question of purpose became more pronounced, higher-stakes. More of us sought meaning beyond the money. I know this from personal experience.

While I was conducting the research for *Leading with Wisdom,* I was teaching an undergraduate course based on what I was learning. Finding purpose was one of the main components of the class, and the topic clearly resonated with students. They dove into class discussions and assignments, and I could tell they appreciated thinking deeply about their own reason for being.

But what is the relationship between our purpose and our work? One of my coaching clients was a successful lawyer who had been diagnosed with a terminal illness. He was seeking advice on what to do now that he couldn't practice law. As I shared all kinds of ideas and options about how he could spend his time, he stopped me and said, "You don't get it. I have worked long enough. I am tired of working."

To which I answered:

> Work is about contribution. It is about a reason for living: the difference you want to make with the rest of your life. Even if you're not going to an office or not earning a paycheck, wanting to contribute is a reason to get up in the morning.

Your reason for getting up in the morning can be called your purpose. Your calling. To use a term we might apply to an organization, it could be your mission. And, as I emphasized to my client, research tells us that people with a strong sense of purpose are mentally and physically healthier than they would be otherwise: they live an average of seven to ten years longer. According to Harvard Medical School, they are more engaged and motivated.

While giving a workshop for mid-level leaders, I explained how I have been going to a monastery for a silent retreat since 2007. This experience, which usually lasts three or four days, is a time to listen to my inner being. It is a time of silence, reflection, and introspection, a time to "hear" what my life is telling me to do.

One of the leaders remarked, "What? I would never want to be alone— with just myself, for days!"

I have never forgotten this comment. If he doesn't want to be with himself, who would want to be with him?

The version of ourselves who shows up at work reflects who we are and how we feel about ourselves. While it is easy to know we need purpose and meaning in our lives, it is harder to make it a reality. As Parker J. Palmer once wrote, "Before I can tell my life what I want to do with it, I must listen to my life telling me who I am."

Breadcrumb Box:

For my podcast, *Becoming a Sage*, I interviewed Tracie Ward, President and Founder of LivingWisely. Her company strives to help individuals and organizations "live your best life on purpose," and she sees legacy as a journey that complements our personal path through life. It is as if the two were "railroad tracks going in the same direction in order to live with greater life intention."

Ward's vision of the legacy journey has three parts. The first third of the journey is focused on the past by understanding our personal history. The second third is focused on the present by reflecting on the past and learning from it to live purposely in the present. The final third—called "generational knowledge"—focuses on the future by teaching and inspiring others and passing forward what we have learned.

Most people share facts, photos, and assets, but not wisdom, knowledge, and values. Yet all that we've learned in the past—if articulated, and passed on—will help us discover our purpose and truly live our legacy.

What Is the Purpose of Purpose?

When we meet someone new, we usually ask: "What do you do?"

While responses can vary, the question usually implies: What kind of *work* do you do? To which we answer, "I'm a teacher." "I'm a doctor." "I'm a banker." "I'm retired."

When my pastor, Wallace Bubar, lived in Germany, he discovered Germans commonly ask a slightly different question: "*Was sind Sie bon Beruf?*" "Beruf" means "calling." So instead of "What do you do?" they ask, "What is your calling in life?" or "What is your vocation?"

Bubar told me that Germans take this concept of vocation seriously. They believe everyone has been called to do something outside of themselves, and find "a deep connection between who you are, spiritually, and the work that you do. You see yourself as involved in some greater purpose."

In our culture, a person's vocation somehow became synonymous with their job title. But vocation is not about goals and accomplishments. It is about where we focus our time and attention.

When we think about finding purpose, it's likely that we're also thinking about finding happiness. A quick Google search reveals that there are more than 23,000 books with the word happiness in the title.

One of these thousands of book is *The How of Happiness: A New Approach to Getting the Life You Want* by Sonja Lyubomirsky. She found that our level of happiness is determined by three factors: 50 percent by one's emotional baseline, 10 percent by one's life circumstances, and 40 percent by "intentional activities," which she defines as events of our choosing—the actions we purposefully seek out.

Put differently, they are intentional breadcrumbs. Habits are repeated behaviors—breadcrumbs—which accumulate into a trail. Lyubomirsky would tell us that being consistent in the breadcrumbs we leave is the key to a life of happiness *and* purpose.

Although happiness, meaning, and purpose are often used interchangeably, they are different. Social psychologist Jennifer Aaker and her colleagues at Stanford University found there are some crucial differences between a happy life and a meaningful life. Distilling their research, here are four main differences:

- Happiness feels good. Meaningfulness doesn't always.
- Happiness is about receiving. Meaningfulness is about giving.
- Happiness is self-focused. Meaningfulness feels bigger than yourself, anchored on others.
- Happiness is fleeting. Meaningfulness is more lasting, and is able to bridge the past, present, and future.

When researchers from the University of Michigan analyzed data from the 27-year-old Health and Retirement Study, they found that only one thing could integrate happiness, fulfillment, and maximum productivity at work: *Living with a sense of purpose and meaning.*

According to research published in *Psychological Science*, when controlled for other factors known to affect longevity (i.e. age, gender, and emotional well-being), a sense of purpose matters more than all of the factors combined. In fact, people with a sense of purpose lived on average 7.5 years longer and had a 15 percent lower risk of death, compared with those who said they were more or less aimless. And it didn't seem to matter when people found their direction. It could be in their 20s, 50s, or 70s.

Purpose is powerful because, according to purposeful living expert Richard Leider, it "is the aim around which we structure our lives, a source of direction and energy. Through the lens of purpose, we are able to see ourselves—and our future—more clearly."

Leider says most people want two things out of life: to belong and to matter. A purpose helps us align our energy and time around specific priorities, and in the ways that are most meaningful.

Breadcrumb Box:

In a webinar sponsored by Wisdom 2.0, CEO and designer Eileen Fisher explained how the coronavirus pandemic gave her a chance to reset both her professional and personal life. While her business was derailed, it was an opportunity to slow down and focus on what was most important.

Fisher said that turned out to be relationships—with family, friends, and co-workers. Although it is easy to get caught up in wanting things to be bigger, better, and faster, the 2020 pandemic reminded her of how precious time is, and how much of a shame it would be to waste it.

She shared her daily dedication to sitting in her "purpose chair" every morning with a cup of coffee in one hand and her journal in the other. This is time for her to set intentions for the day and ground her in what's important each morning.

Finding Your Purpose

Daniel Goleman, one of the authorities on Emotional Intelligence, defines purpose as our intentions in action, which goes beyond self-interest. "If we find purpose in helping people, or some goal toward a greater good, it gives us a sense of wellbeing no matter what else may happen," he explains.

Our intentions help create our life story: What makes your heart sing? And how can you make intentional actions an essential part of your day?

"Purpose" can sound like a lofty goal, and is often misunderstood. Of course, it can mean completely different things to different people. Most assume that purpose is simply the degree to which you feel connected to something "bigger than yourself." However, those who feel they have purpose in their life don't always feel *Purpose* with a big P. Instead, they might *purpose*, with a little p, in small ways: through breadcrumbs.

Purpose can be as simple as focusing on one's family. It could be a bigger P, such as contributing to societal causes. It could also be more focused on personal growth through learning new skills. Your purpose can change depending on your age, your stage of life, the context of your situation. As we grow and evolve, so can purpose. Ordinary, but consistent actions and interactions on a daily basis can have meaning.

It is one thing to talk about purpose, but it is another to actually discover our purpose. One way to find our purpose is to ask *why* several times. According to Goleman, we can discover our purpose by reflecting on what we have done and asking "why." *Why did I do that?* After you answer, repeat the process: ask "why" again, until we get to the heart of our actions.

Here are a few examples from my own life:

Q: Why are you a hospice volunteer?
A: Because I wanted to learn more about compassion.
Q: Why do you want to learn about compassion?
A: Because embracing death and dying is part of positive aging.
Q: Why is embracing death part of positive aging?

A: Death can happen at any time, so we are reminded to live each day on purpose.

Since we can make "purpose" too complex, Leider has a simple formula he calls the napkin test because you literally could draft it on a napkin. He advocates starting with this equation:

Gifts + Passions + Values = Calling (purpose)

Gifts: Natural talents. Can't remember learning it. Enjoy doing it. Others observe it in you. Find out *how* you want to help.

Passions: Interests. Curiosities. Causes. What keeps you up at night? Find out *who* you want to help.

Values: What do you stand for? What is important to you? Find out *what* energizes you and drains you.

If a purpose is about using our gifts, passions, and values to benefit something beyond ourselves, then what holds us back from finding our purpose? Leider believes there are four major purpose "myths":

1 To have purpose means doing something original.
2 Only a few special people have true purpose in their lives, such as Mother Teresa.
3 True purpose comes as inspiration or revelation.
4 Purpose is a luxury and most people don't have time for it.

Letting go of these purpose myths empowers us to search for it in our own life.

If you are struggling to discover a purpose, Leider suggests using this Default Purpose: To Grow and To Give. He advocates writing it on a Post-it Note on the bathroom mirror as a friendly, daily reminder.

As is often the case with legacy, it is natural to assume that a purpose needs to be some Earth-moving mission. But it can be as simple as reflecting on this question at the end of the day: How did I grow and give today?

Breadcrumb Box:

Marshall Goldsmith defines the "good life" using six variables:

1. Purpose: Doing something valuable
2. Progress: Achievement
3. Happiness and joy in the process of progress
4. Meaning

5. Relationships
6. Engagement in the Present

"None of these guarantees any of the others," he noted. "Happiness and meaning need to happen together."

To stay true to these variables, relationships are important. Goldsmith meets weekly with 50 other people devoted to living out these principles of the good life. "We try to help each other: How'd you do this week?"

Another one of Goldsmith's breadcrumbs is his email closing. In each message, he closes with the same phrase, "Life is good." Based on my interactions with Goldsmith, he believes this and wants to share the feeling.

Finding Your Why

Based on the work of Simon Sinek, "Fulfillment starts with understanding exactly *why* we do what we do."

Dave Evans and Bob Burnett's book, *Designing Your Life: How to Build a Well-Lived Joyful Life* grew out of their experiences teaching the Design Program at Stanford. They believe people need a "design process for figuring out what they want, whom they want to grow into, and how to create a life they love." The design process by Evans and Burnett is another way to discover your purpose or to find your WHY.

While happiness is often fleeting and self-focused, meaning involves investing in something bigger than yourself—which tells us that a meaningful life often includes stress, effort, struggle, and challenge. In a survey of over 2 million people in more than 500 jobs by the organization PayScale, those who reported finding the most meaning and purpose in their careers were clergy, teachers, and surgeons—difficult jobs that don't always cultivate happiness in the moment, but ones that contribute to society and foster a sense of purpose.

In one large-scale study reported in *Harvard Business Review* in 2015, 80 percent of CEOs declared that purpose is important for their organizations, but fewer than 50 percent of those organizations leverage purpose in an impactful way.

Stanford professor Jennifer Aaker argues in her book *The Dragonfly Effect* that this is because few leaders know how to think about purpose in a clear way; some see it as an individual concern, while others associate it with philanthropy. This prevents them from encouraging their companies to work toward a purpose collectively, let alone effectively.

The reality is that developing purpose is much more of a skill than we think. Although many people feel that purpose is static—something that is defined by their workplace, their boss, or even their spouse—it can be defined by individuals, like you, if given the right tools.

Breadcrumb Box:

Ayse Birsel, author of *Design the Life You Love: A Step-by-Step Guide to Building a Meaningful Life,* has been designing award-winning products for over 20 years. During the financial crisis, she decided to focus her time and energy applying the same design concepts for her furniture to designing life.

The result was her book and acclaimed workshops. Birsel told me she welcomes people aged 9–90+ to her workshops because "people of all ages want the same thing—love, friendships, well-being, and purpose." She explained how kids leave home and people retire, but the need for purpose is constant regardless of our age.

Legacy is a powerful tool: as Birsel said, it is about "making meaning out of life." The challenge is finding ways to give form to our experiences to share them with other people—it can "teach the next generation to fall in love with what you are doing so that they want to keep it alive." Marshall Goldsmith, for example, took Birsel's ideas to heart, and dedicated himself to leaving behind a meaningful professional legacy. For others, legacy might be focused on family and friends. But we all have something to share.

Birsel believes legacy creation is a product, process, habit, or tradition. When I asked her why she uses the word "design" instead of "re-design," she explained that circumstances constantly change, offering us new ingredients to work with. "People need guidance and tools to make designing easier," she explained. "At the end of the day, it is about creating joy and making time and space for what matters most."

As she optimistically and hopefully put it, "Our life is our biggest project."

Dreams versus Goals

Several years ago, I read *The Dream Manager* by Matthew Kelly. It is a short, fictional story about creating a workplace culture where people *want* to work.

A "Dream Manager" helps employees put together a plan to achieve their dreams. They meet regularly to assess their progress and discuss next steps. They discover that helping employees move in the direction of their dreams creates a dynamic workplace and adds value to their lives both professionally and personally.

A couple of years ago, I participated in a webinar and one of the participants from Indiana shared that she was a Dream Manager. It is one thing to read about it in a book, but I wanted to talk with an actual Dream Manager!

So I called one up—we'll call her "Joyce," who worked at Goodwill Industries International.

Joyce completed the Matthew Kelly certification because Goodwill Industries International is a strong believer in the program. She considered listening to employees' dreams and helping them develop a plan for reaching them the most rewarding part of her position.

Reading this simple book had a profound effect on me. What is the difference between striving for dreams and accomplishing goals? Do we know the dreams of the people we care about including family members? How would relationships be different if we knew and cared about their dreams?

We encourage our kids to dream and think big. We talk to young people about reaching for the stars. But with age and experience, we seem to stop dreaming. While dreams are invisible, they are powerful. We get focused on getting things done, being busy, having healthcare coverage, and making mortgage payments. We tend to forget about reaching for our dreams. We may not even have any dreams for ourselves anymore.

In my workshops, I ask participants to share a few of their dreams. Then I ask them to talk about their goals. There is an observable difference. People are much more energized, inspired, and engaged when talking about their dreams versus their goals.

After reading Kelly's book, I shared my dreams with my husband and sons, and asked them about their own. Now that we know each other's dreams, we can work to support each other while pursuing them.

By describing our dreams to the people we care about, they will move from thoughts to true possibilities—and we'll help others' dreams become more real in the same way.

The Power of Rituals

At work, purpose is associated with positive outcomes such as productivity, job satisfaction, growth and development, and retention. If deliberate habits are important to happiness, they are also important to purpose.

According to a McKinsey report, it's much more likely that executives will feel connected to their organization's purpose than lower-level employees. It's up to leaders to fix this: 63 percent of people wished their employer would create opportunities to find purpose in their day-to-day work. Employees who feel invested in their company's purpose are more likely to work harder, with more inspiration for innovation.

When I interviewed Erica Keswin, author of *Rituals Roadmap: The Human Way to Transform Everyday Routines into Workplace Magic*, she told me that leaders can start by recognizing the importance of rituals. These are meaningful events that take place regularly, but have a deeper importance than habits or routines.

In Keswin's view, a ritual consists of three Ps: psychological safety, purpose, and performance. When people feel safe and are invested in the purpose in what they are doing, their performance increases.

These rituals can *connect* employees to their company's values. When individuals work alongside team members with a shared mission, they naturally feel in sync with each other. All the more reason for leaders to align their workplace calendar with a common mission.

Along those lines, Aaker's research indicates greater profits result when the purpose of an organization is clear because it drives engagement, productivity, and retention. She points to the way that John Mackey at Whole Foods has emphasized the need for organizations to stand for something for a long time. In his view, a CEO should be a servant leader, and if an organization maximizes purpose, the profits will follow.

Aaker considered the success of brands that have leveraged purpose: Apple has marketed themselves on minimalistic efficiency, Lululemon on empowerment, Google on truth. Patagonia is another company that has been on the purpose journey for years. Similarly, Tom's of Maine, Tom's Shoes, and Timberland have been recognized as purpose-focused.

Purpose is crucial for organizations, since it helps to attract and retain employees. Furthermore, rituals can be used to reinforce purpose. Keswin advised me:

> Think about how to use rituals to honor relationships—with your colleagues, with your boss, with your customers, with your friends and family. But, most importantly, think about how to honor that relationship with yourself. To put your oxygen mask on first, as hard as it might be sometimes.

Breadcrumb Box:

When I asked Howard Behar, former president of Starbucks Coffee Company International, to define servant leader, he provided this personal example:

> You have to really know yourself and your values. Start with the idea that everything you do can be a conscious decision with confidence. I wrote down my values and I have it in my briefcase that I carry with me. I've carried this with me for 50 years! It includes my 10 core values, my mission statement, and my guiding principles of how I want to live my life.
>
> You might ask why I have to carry them around with me. Well, because in times of stress it is easy to get off track. I want a constant reminder and if you don't write it down then it isn't worth much and doesn't add much value to your life.

The Power of Showing Up

My clients and friends often don't know where to start to find their purpose. The easy answer is to explore, experiment, and discover.

A good way to judge whether you find purpose at work is to assess whether you are using *unique strengths*, whether you are *passionate about what you do,* and whether you feel you are *working on a worthy challenge.*

If you answered "no" to one or more of these questions, don't despair. Purpose is a process: as you feel yourself working toward it, you are actually cultivating it within yourself.

Chip Conley, the author of this book's Foreword as well as the author of *Wisdom@Work* and of the blog *Wisdom Well,* breaks down the definition of "purpose" in a memorable way. "As a noun, it's something you possess—a valued asset in your grasp that you can show to others," he says. "But, as a verb, it's a deliberate and conscious way of being...It's much like happiness, always better when it arrives organically and on its own time, rather than being pursued."

By orienting ourselves toward meaning and purpose, we no longer see happiness as an ultimate goal we are always striving to reach. Rather, we reinforce daily connections between happiness, meaning, and purpose.

So, when you are thinking about purpose, ask yourself how you might be of service to someone beyond yourself. Conley says that when we do this, we "move into that action-minded, verb-focused approach to purpose, and you may soon find unexpected gifts coming [your] way."

Individuals who think of purpose as a verb will become happier, and the organizations that adopt this philosophy will have a very different metric of success. They can do this by coalescing around an inspired collective mission, or collaborating to unlock that purpose in each individual. At that point, work and life can blend fluidly together and take you on a journey—one that's captured in stories, shifting in chapters, and guided by purpose.

Back to the movie *About Schmidt.* While there are some humorous scenes in the film, I left the theater feeling melancholy. But it also set me on a quest to live my future differently than Warren Schmidt and to help others do the same.

Breadcrumb Box:

One spring break we took a family vacation to Hawaii.

When we were walking on the beach in Waikiki, we came upon a few people hand-crafting items out of palm leaves to sell. One man's work caught my attention. He was making bowls, but I wanted a larger one than what he had available.

He said if I paid him $10, I could come back later that day to pick it up. I told him I could return the next day, but I could not come back that day. "Why not?" he asked. I explained how I had a spa appointment and then I had to meet my family, and after that, I had to be somewhere else at a certain time.

"Lady, you are too busy," he responded. "You need to slow down. You should be relaxing. Look at the ocean. I get to see it every day."

I went back the next day to pick up the bowl. Call me naive, but I assumed he was an artist when he was actually homeless and living on the beach. He was happy and relaxed.

He reminded me that it's easier to fill our time than fulfilling our time. He was telling me how to live. *Don't be so busy that you're not appreciating what's directly in front of you.*

Breadcrumb Ingredients for Cultivating Purpose

Discover and Explore:

Learn an instrument, volunteer, or take a leadership role for a cause you support. Attend college classes in subjects that now stimulate your mind, such as history, writing, or science. Or focus on new skills, such as public speaking, painting, cooking, or auto repair.

If you need further inspiration, go back to your youth. What sports, hobbies, or activities did you enjoy when you were younger? Why not try them again?

Peeling the Onion:

Who are you? Ask yourself once, then write down your response. After that? Ask yourself again. Repeat the process five times to get to a deeper level—the core—of who you really are.

"The Box of Unlived Life":

Imagine that you have a "box of unlived life," almost like a time capsule from the future that you're meant to open later in life. Perhaps it contains untapped possibilities from earlier in your life, or an interest you were always curious about exploring, or a different sense of your purpose from when you were younger.

What is in this box? And once you grasp whatever it is that feels "unlived," how can you help yourself explore that life today? Again, think in terms of everyday actions.

Bibliography

Aaker, J., Smith, A., & Adler, C. (2010). *The dragonfly effect: Quick, effective, and powerful ways to use social media to drive social change*. San Francisco, CA: Jossey-Bass.

Birsel, A. (2015). *Design the life you love: A step-by-step guide to building a meaningful life*. Berkeley, CA: Ten Speed Press.

Conley, C. (2018). *Wisdom@Work. The making of a modern elder*. New York: Currency.

Dahl, M. (June 7, 2016). "The only person who can make your job meaningful is you." *The Cut*. http://nymag.com/scienceofus/2016/06/your-boss-cant-make-your-job-meaningful-for-you.html

Evans, D. & Burnett, R. (2016). *Designing your life: How to build a well-lived joyful life*. New York: Alfred A. Knopf.

Fisher, E. (June 11, 2021). *Community and connection in mid-life and beyond*. [Video]. *YouTube*. https://youtu.be/FFgWOpmYVWE

Freed, J. E. (2013). *Leading with wisdom: Sage advice from 100 experts*. Alexandria, VA: ATD.

Goleman, D. (March 3, 2021). Purpose, wellbeing, and achievement. Emotional Intelligence with Daniel Goleman. https://www.linkedin.com/pulse/purpose-wellbeing-achievement-daniel-goleman/?trk=eml-email_series_follow_newsletter_01-hero-1-title_link&midToken=AQGqNLaNI5ljMw&-fromEmail=fromEmail&ut=18WgxviMFFJpE1

Goleman, D. (n.d.). *Millennials: The purpose generation*. Los Angeles, CA: Korn Ferry. https://www.kornferry.com/insights/this-week-in-leadership/millennials-purpose-generation

Hill, P. L. & Turiano, N. A. (May 8, 2014). Purpose in life as a predictor of mortality across adulthood. *Psychological Science, 25*(7), 1482–1486. https://journals.sagepub.com/doi/abs/10.1177/0956797614531799

Kelly, M. (2015). *The dream manager*. Westport, SD: Hyperion.

Leider, R. J. & Shapiro, D. A. (2021). *Who do you want to be when you grow old? The path of purposeful aging*. Oakland, CA: Berrett-Koehler, Inc.

Lyubomirsky, S. (2008). *The how of happiness: A new approach to getting the life you want*. New York: The Penguin Press.

Mautz, S. (August 14, 2019). "A 27-year study says 1 thing is key to happiness and longevity in work and life." *Inc.* https://www.inc.com/scott-mautz/a-27-year-study-says-1-thing-is-key-to-happiness-longevity-in-work-life.html

Payne, A. (Director). (2002). *About Schmidt* [Film]. New Line Cinema.

Sinek, S. (2011). *Start with WHY: How great leaders inspire everyone to take action*. New York: Portfolio/Penguin.

Stafford, W. (1999). *The way it is: New and selected poems*. Minneapolis, MN: Graywolf Press.

Chapter 3

Drop Your Tools

Several years ago, a keynote speaker at the Organizational Behavior Teaching Conference made a significant impression on me. During COVID-19, his message was a mantra I heard repeatedly in my head: "Drop your tools!"

The speaker was Karl Weick, Professor of Organizational Behavior and Psychology at the University of Michigan. Using real-world examples, he built a case that educators can be better prepared to meet these challenges if they *drop their tools*—that is, let go of familiar strategies and embrace the unknown.

Weick studied wildland firefighters and discovered at least 23 had died in four separate incidents since 1990 with their tools next to them—always within sight of safety zones that, if they had less to carry, they could have reached. If only they had dropped their tools.

He also studied fighter pilots and found that those "whose planes become disabled lose their lives when they hold onto what they call 'the cocoon of the cockpit' rather than face the conditions of ejection from the aircraft." And while NASA was assessing the damage of the Columbia shuttle disaster, their final report noted that "NASA management was not able to recognize that in unprecedented conditions when lives are on the line, flexibility and democratic process should take priority over bureaucratic response."

"Learning to drop one's tools to gain lightness, agility, and wisdom tends to be forgotten in an era where leaders and followers alike are preoccupied with knowledge management, acquisitions, and acquisitiveness," Weick observed. "Nevertheless, human potential is realized as much by what we drop, as what we acquire."

According to Carol Dweck in her book *Mindset: The Psychology of Success*, we can navigate life using one of two mindsets: fixed and growth. With a fixed mindset, we try to *prove* ourselves; since success is about winning, we are less likely to take risks. With a growth mindset, we try to *improve* ourselves, and view success as a process of learning. This makes us more open to taking calculated risks.

When times are challenging and change is accelerating, we need to "drop our tools" in order to be innovative and resilient. Doing so takes a growth mindset.

DOI: 10.4324/9781003310211-3

Reimagine. Reset.

The early stages of the pandemic triggered a collective mourning for all that we had lost. But, to persevere, we sought silver linings in both life and work.

Whether you're making decisions for your company or thinking ahead in your personal life, the main questions we must confront are: What do we want to hold onto? And what do we want to—*need* to—let go of in order to function in the future?

What many people call pivoting, I call dropping your tools. This involves letting go of systems, processes, practices, and mindsets that no longer serve you or the organization. Again, this requires embracing a growth mindset.

Anne-Marie Slaughter, CEO of New America, pointed out in an article in the *New York Times* how quickly some industries and governments, many resistant to change, were able to "drop their tools" and realize positive outcomes to survive during the pandemic. Colleges and universities moved all of their classes online in a short period of time. Churches moved their services online.

Even my local yoga studio, which closed during lockdown, was able to maintain and grow its business over Zoom. Now my yoga instructor/owner isn't tied to a fixed, physical location. He can scale his business and reduce his overhead in a way that was previously impossible.

When leaders are not bound by the fixed mindsets of the past, they can harness a growth mindset to drop tools that no longer serve them. This will encourage employees to innovate and adapt to change. That way, everyone can respond more quickly and think more creatively about newer, better practices that will better serve others going forward.

Change Your Mindset, Change Your World

Becoming a good person and good leader involves accepting who we are, where we are in life, and how we view the world. Our perspective affects how we see ourselves, how we see others, and the breadcrumbs we leave.

Yet, our mindsets sometimes *don't* help us do our best work and live our best lives. These mindsets are the "tools" we may need to drop in order to be faster, more agile, able to pivot, and open to continual growth.

Ellen Langer, the Harvard psychology professor who is known as the mother of mindfulness, also believes that a rigid mindset can hold us back. She defines mindfulness as the "simple process of noticing new things" which results in improved health, competence, and happiness. But, frequently, she says most of us are *mindless*.

When we drop our "tools," we are allowed to be curious and creative—which allows us to be open to the possibilities of each moment. Similarly, Langer believes every moment is a wakeup call: breadcrumbs we should be actively noticing.

This is why mindfulness has become a popular leadership topic and practice. The moments leaders notice are reflections of their mindfulness: these are the opportunities they sense to make a difference, large or small. These "noticeable" moments influence our impact in the workplace and in all that we do.

Richard Leider uses the metaphor of "unpacking and repacking our bags" to think about our life journey. As we travel along our paths, what should we keep in our bags? Should we be unpacking and leaving things behind? And how should we repack our bags to prepare for the journey before us?

What "tools" do we need to drop because they no longer serve us?

Breadcrumb Box:

Julia Storberg-Walker, a professor at George Washington University in the Department of Human and Organizational Learning, shared this story with me:

> My first career was as a global consultant at Deloitte. I was unconscious of my values. We called ourselves "insecure overachievers." The goal was to climb the ladder and get ahead and the reward system reinforced this behavior. I was doing what I thought I was supposed to do.
>
> Then I began to have doubts. I called them "drops of grace" that came raining down on me and compelled me to make a change. One 'drop' I remember well. I was in a limousine from the airport taking me to my hotel and this thought came into my head from out of nowhere. The cost of this limo would buy a lot of books for inner-city schools. This made me realize I wasn't being a whole person when I went to work. I had to make a change when I went to work.

Storberg-Walker concluded,

> Life is the practice. We play out who we are in moments. We want our highest nature to come through. My mission is to teach leadership wisdom instead of skills and competencies. This means body knowing and heart knowing is as important as intellectual knowing. Healing would be an important component of this leadership wisdom. I teach this through reflective and contemplative practices such as mindfulness.

Abundance, Not Scarcity

If you are going to be the best person you can be, then it is important to be comfortable with who you are and the wisdom you have to offer. This involves having a healthy ego, one which does not control you.

A healthy ego helps us embrace, appreciate, and show gratitude toward every phase of life. It helps us live in the present without regretting the past or fearing the future. We need to face the fact that 70 is not the new 50, and 60 is not the new 40, and 50 is not the new 30. Seventy is the new 70. I end each of my podcast interviews with my mantra and tagline: *May the rest of life be the best of life.*

Dr. Elmer Burack, my professional mentor, encouraged me in 2007 to get involved with Sage-ing International. He sent me the book *From Aging to Sage-ing: A Profound New Vision to Growing Older* by Zalman Schachter-Shalomi. "Baby boomers are not going to know what to do with themselves after they retire," he told me. "Since we are living longer, people will need help navigating this new territory. I think this could be your calling."

Gaining a certification as a Sage-ing Leader was the beginning of my life journey toward becoming a better person. One of the main components of Sage-ing is to challenge Western society's love affair with youth.

Ageism seems to be the last "ism" that many people don't dispute. And yet, we are fortunate if we're able to go through the process of aging. Sage-ing frames aging as a time to become whole people (not old people) and to gain wisdom.

A study conducted by researchers at Yale and the University of Miami revealed that middle-aged adults who viewed aging positively lived 7.5 years longer than those with more negative perceptions of it. Your mindset can even prolong your life.

If we shift our perspective in this way, then we will also undergo a related shift in mindset, from scarcity to abundance. With a scarcity mindset, people see life as a finite pie—which can make the process of aging feel like time is running out. But with a mindset of abundance, there is plenty of pie to go around. In fact, the pie can get bigger, and still provide new opportunities to learn.

The corporate world tends to reinforce a scarcity mentality. When resources are limited, competition rules: survival of the fittest. When promotions and raises are scarce, managers hoard information, micromanagement abounds, and generally, short-term thinking is the norm. Instead, embracing an abundance mindset requires we move away from *competition* into *cooperation and collaboration.*

Parker J. Palmer, prominent author and founder and Senior Partner Emeritus of the Center for Courage and Renewal, integrated his humility with his abundance mindset. He told me he learned the value of legacy from his dad, who demonstrated daily acts of kindness.

"He talked to people in airports who would be cleaning the restrooms," Palmer remembered. "He would tip them, thank them, and move on. He believed in spreading wealth. What you give away, you receive over and over again," Palmer concluded. "Too many people understand the price of everything and the value of nothing."

Working across Generations

We need to celebrate the sum of our life experiences and pass on what we've learned. This can be done through mentoring others, teaching, writing memoirs or books. In fact, intergenerational learning is key to conscious aging.

Chip Conley, author of *Wisdom@Work*, mentored Brian Chesky, the founder of Airbnb. Through this experience, Conley learned that each generation has strengths, but can learn so much from each other. Through intergenerational mentoring, older workers can teach how to build relationships and manage emotions. Younger workers can teach how to best utilize technology for efficiency. Conley calls this exchange trading EQ (emotional intelligence) for DQ (digital intelligence).

This calls to mind an insight from my interview with Peter Senge, senior lecturer at the MIT Sloan School of Management and author of the classic book *The Fifth Discipline: The Art & Practice of the Learning Organization*. I told him I was interviewing wise sages to learn best how to prepare people to be effective leaders, and he said I was onto something. He added, "Just being older does not make someone wiser."

The mindsets we use to see life can either hold us back or propel us forward. When we "drop our tools," we become better people—better leaders. We are mindful when we are conscious of the crumbs we are leaving behind. We have a growth mindset when we continue to learn, grow, and contribute in ways that make our life worth remembering.

Conley believes wisdom entails recognizing patterns in life. And the older you are, the more patterns you've seen. An African proverb states, "When an elder dies, it's like a library has burned down." Regardless of our age, our personal treasure chests of information, knowledge, and wisdom need to be shared so that they are not lost. And wisdom never grows old.

Breadcrumb Box:

We can be role models for others by "dropping our tools" and other mindsets pushed upon us by the media and society. A few years ago, I was facilitating a leadership workshop for women CPAs. One participant's story stood out:

> My grandmother is a Sage. She is living life the way I admire. I asked her how she figured life out and she told me she has always had a role model—someone she admires. About every decade she selects a person who is living a life that is attractive to her and she follows her lead.

How You Show Up Matters

We touched on this briefly in Chapter 2, but it bears repeating. After interviewing many leaders, a common theme emerged: how you show up matters.

In the context of the mindsets we've been discussing, "showing up" is about presence. It's not only about the way people experience *you*, but it's also about how others experience *themselves* when in your presence.

Rob Salafia, author of *Leading from Your Best Self: Develop Executive Poise, Presence, and Influence to Maximize Your Potential*, describes showing up this way:

> It matters how you show up. Poise, presence, and how you build relationships is part of who you are. The way you show up has an impact on others and how they show up. How you breathe, walk, speak, your tone of voice matters. It is a vibrational thing that transfers to others unconsciously.

Salafia also told me that presence is a choice: "You build your legacy a piece at a time (breadcrumbs) and it accumulates. It is better to be conscious about what you are leaving."

In other words, the way we show up might require us to drop our tools. Salafia suggested we ask these questions of ourselves:

- What's the part of yourself that you left behind to be the person you are today?
- What is the best version of yourself?
- As you look to the future, what's the part of yourself you have to let go of to become your best future self?
- At the end of life, the person you became meets the person you could have become. What do they say to each other?

Barbara Beizer is a leadership, transition, and life coach. While working with people over 50, she's noticed that their achievements focus more on the kind of person they want to be. "We move from an external presence to an internal one, which creates a different presence in the world," she explained, adding that an internal focus creates more empathy and understanding.

Basically, Beizer is talking about how we show up. To become more intentional about how we do so, she suggested asking yourself these questions:

- What is my legacy so far?
- How might I shape it in the future?
- Is the mold set, or is it malleable?

She uses this summarizing question to guide her work: "What will help you become the person you want to be and achieve whatever you want to achieve?"

Leadership consultant Sally Helgesen stressed another aspect of showing up. "We demonstrate leadership through explicit *practices*," she explained. In our conversation, she shared two simple but powerful stories about what this might look like:

> I had the opportunity to shadow Frances Hesselbein when she was the CEO of Girl Scouts of America. She was going to be interviewed by a *New York Times* reporter. Prior to the call, she sent out a message (before the internet) to invite five young people from the media and communications department to sit in her office while she made the call.
>
> They had no role to play, but to listen. After the interview, I asked Frances the purpose of inviting these young people to sit in for the conversation. She said, "I want them to see how it's done. They'll remember."

How many people at a young age get to "see" how it is done?

People will remember the level of attention and care you demonstrate toward others. We often say repeated behaviors become habits. And our habits inform the way we show up each day.

Helgesen's second story also proved this point:

> Peter Drucker had a practice of always speaking last in any meeting. He knew his power and he wanted to hear what others had to say. This was part of his legacy. He understood the power of listening.

Helgesen's stories illustrate how these practices almost become policies—they serve the greater good. These practices also help train future leaders. Above all, Helgesen noted that both Hesselbein and Drucker "had a heightened 'legacy awareness' of kindness and generosity. They demonstrated humility and patience, which were really gifts to others."

Todd Cherches, author of *VisuaLeadership: Leveraging the Power of Visual Thinking in Leadership and Life,* told me what showing up means to him. He teaches graduate students and his coaching clients about the 3 Vs: visibility, voice, and value. How are you seen by others? How are you heard by others? How are you giving or adding value?

As he put it, "Legacy is how you are perceived by others—your current personal brand."

How do you really know how others perceive you? Sometimes you don't know until it is too late. Cherches uses the metaphor of the "fun house mirror" to describe how your self-perception is often distorted. Your self-insight may or may not be accurate. But by listening to external insights from people we trust, we'll gain self-awareness.

Breadcrumb Box:

My interviews revealed several examples of how showing up can leave behind breadcrumbs:

- "Paying attention gets attention."—Deborah James, Former United States Secretary of the Air Force and the second woman to lead the country's military service
- "Don't listen to what I say. Watch what I do."—Jack Maguire, Chair and Founder of Maguire Associates
- "Smiling can be a breadcrumb moment."—Tim Hebert, CEO of Trilix
- "I try to write every email with love and energy going through it."—Judi Neal, founder and CEO of Edgewalkers International
- "We leave our imprint everywhere and every day."—Suzanne Bates, Founder and Managing Director of BTS Boston
- "Be fundamentally curious. Every person we meet has value and is worthy of compassion." —Susan McPherson, CEO of McPherson Strategies
- "We should operate from a place of generosity, grace, and gratitude: having the disposition to do something more for others."—Todd Cherches, executive coach and CEO/Co-Founder of BigBlueGumball

Rethink. Reframe.

As Weick taught me, gaining wisdom is about dropping whatever is not serving you well. Let go of stereotypes that box you in and limit your potential.

To do this, abandon fixed and scarcity mindsets. Neither mindset encourages you to be your best self. We have a tendency to hang onto what we know, but this inhibits growth and learning.

Instead, when we adopt growth and abundance mindsets, we are better able to live the lives for which we want to be remembered. We create situations where everyone can win and thrive, not just survive. Leadership expert Jim Kouzes told me his goal is to get out of bed, put his feet on the ground, and say, "Today is a good day to have a good day."

Breadcrumb Ingredients for Dropping Your Tools

Mirror, Mirror on the Wall:

Be aware of the story you have in your own head about yourself. Now, confront that story by looking at your own face in the mirror.

Study your reaction. What do you see in your own face? Should you drop the narrative you hold onto about yourself? Does your impression of that story change as you examine your reflection?

Drop the Judgment:

Imagine your thoughts are totally transparent. If they were, would you think awful things about other people? Try to find a way to understand their perspective by asking questions rather than jumping to an unfair and judgemental assumption.

Create an Ignorance List:

What do you want to know more about? Where and how can you learn what you want to know?

Create a Stop-Doing List and a To-Learn List:

We may need to actively change our habits to make room to learn something new. Since we only have 24 hours in a day, create a "stop-doing" list to create that time. Write down the tasks that get in the way of experiencing something new or gaining positive skills.

Bibliography

Cherches, T. (2020). *VisuaLeadership: Leveraging the power of visual thinking in leadership and life*. New York: Post Hill Press.

Conley, C. (April 18, 2017). "I joined Airbnb at 52, and here's what I learned about age, wisdom, and the tech industry." *Harvard Business Review*. https://hbr.org/2017/04/i-joined-airbnb-at-52-and-heres-what-i-learned-about-age-wisdom-and-the-tech-industry

Dweck, C. (2007). *Mindset: The new psychology of success*. New York: Ballantine Books.

Langer, E. (March, 2014). "Mindfulness in the age of complexity." *Harvard Business Review*. https://hbr.org/2014/03/mindfulness-in-the-age-of-complexity

Leider, R. J. & Shapiro, D. A. *Repacking your bags: Lighten your load for the good life*. San Francisco, CA: Berrett-Koehler Publishing, Inc.

Levy, B. R., Slade, M. D., Kunkel, S. R., & Kasl, S. V. (2002). "Longevity increased by positive self-perceptions of aging." *Journal of Personality and Social Psychology*, 83(2), 261–270. https://doi.org/10.1037//0022-3514.83.2.261

Salafia, R. (2018). *Leading from your best self: Develop executive poise, presence, and influence to maximize your potential.* New York: McGraw-Hill Education.

Schachter-Shalomi, Z. & Miller, R. S. (1995). *From aging to sage-ing: A profound new vision to growing older.* New York: Grand Central Publishing. https://pubmed.ncbi.nlm.nih.gov/12150226/

Slaughter, A. M. (March 21, 2020). "Forget the Trump administration. America will save America." *The New York Times.* https://www.nytimes.com/2020/03/21/opinion/sunday/coronavirus-governors-cities.html

Weick, K. (2007). "Drop your tools: On reconfiguring management education," *Journal of Management Education*, 31(1), 5–16.

Chapter 4

Become a Nobody

Several years ago, I was at the Sage-ing International Conference having lunch with expert on aging Harry "Rick" Moody, author of *The Five Stages of the Soul*. When we were talking about ego, Rick said, "The goal is to become a nobody."

When I asked Rick what he meant, he explained that the first half of life is about accomplishments. Getting an education, climbing the corporate ladder, raising a family. In these stages of life, we try to become a "some-body," or at least ourselves. But the second half of life is about letting go of your ego and becoming a nobody, a term popularized by Ram Dass (Richard Alpert). In fact, a 2019 documentary about Ram Dass was titled *Becoming Nobody*.

In *Becoming Nobody*, director Jamie Catto integrates archival clips into an engaging conversation between him and Ram Dass. The film helps us understand how our old roles and disguises become increasingly burdensome—even before COVID-19, they were masks that we had to take off.

The film captures a loving man full of joy, wit, honesty, and wisdom, comfortable sharing his considerable pains and pleasures throughout his life. Ram Dass explains how his life experiences freed him from the at-tachments of his "somebody-ness" and transformed him into a soul who now inspires a new generation. To overcome that somebody-ness, Ram Dass pointed to the title of his book, *Be Here Now*: "In each moment, go into the moment. Our minds take us back and forth in time."

According to Ram Dass, Western life makes spiritual development difficult. "Thoughts, thoughts, thoughts: Those are the daily attention-grabbers that make it so that you can't come from your mind to your heart to your soul," he once said. "The soul contains love, compassion, wisdom, peace, and joy, but more people identify with the mind. You're not an ego. You're a soul."

Personally, I find the writings of Ram Dass complicated to understand. But after my research, I concluded he is basically saying we need to shift

DOI: 10.4324/9781003310211-4

from focusing on our roles in life (what we do) to our soul (who we are). It is easy to identify with what we do in life.

When I interviewed executive coach Dan Petersen for my book *Leading with Wisdom,* he shared a definition of ego that I have always remembered. "The ego is the difference between what you want to have happen and what is happening," he observed. "It is the gap between what we want and what is. When we learn to 'let go' of the difference, we are controlling the ego and not letting it control us."

Right now, you may be thinking: isn't it important to become a "somebody" to find our true purpose? In fact, these are two different processes: becoming a nobody will bring you closer to self-actualization. We may know what we *want* in life, but the ego makes it hard to focus on what *matters* most.

In *Man's Search for Meaning,* Viktor Frankl discusses how a lifelong path toward meaning consists of choices, decisions, and consequences. When I read the book for the first time, I wanted to underline almost every sentence. For me, the most powerful quote is: "Everything can be taken from a man but one thing: the last of the human freedoms—to choose one's attitude in any given set of circumstances, to choose one's own way."

But our ego can make it hard to stay on the right track and to do the right thing. It is easy to get caught up in competition, or in needlessly comparing ourselves with others.

In his book *The Road to Character,* David Brooks distinguishes between résumé virtues and eulogy virtues. Résumé virtues include extrinsic rewards: the things we have done to climb the ladder or accomplishments we can list on our résumés. They tend to focus on the *what* questions, which appeal to our ego: *What do you do? What do you own? What do you drive? What do others think of you?*

Breadcrumb Box:

Jim Autry, former Fortune 500 executive, believes "the greatest enemy for people is ego." He said we need to use compassion and empathy to overcome an ego that wants to control us. These values guide us toward understanding the other person rather than trying to compete with them.

"We often follow the wrong role models," Autry explained. "We have failed to shut up and listen. We often fail to think deeply before we act … There seems to be an obsession with self and money—too much emphasis on developing our own personal brand and influencers. The real influencers should be servant leaders who embrace relationships, are supportive and compassionate, yet accountable."

Eulogy virtues, however, run deeper. These are virtues that reflect your character, the ones people would recall at your funeral or celebration of life. This might sound familiar from what we've learned so far about legacy. These attributes concern your being. They tend to focus on the *who* questions: *Who are you? Who did you become? Who did you influence during your life?*

The Ego

As I was thinking about the power of the ego, I was reminded of Max Ehrmann's early 1920s prose poem "Desiderata." I first discovered it in college, and was so mesmerized that I memorized it in full. Later on, I incorporated it into postcards that I include with graduation gifts.

In the poem, Ehrmann reminds us to keep our ego in check because we live in a competitive culture: "... If you compare yourself with others, you may become vain and bitter. For always there will be greater and lesser persons than yourself."

Consider the importance of sports in our society. Although they teach many good virtues—teamwork, competition, interdependence, and the value of practice—they still sort people into winners and losers. This attitude can carry over into all aspects of life: Who is thinner? Smarter? Richer? Faster? The list goes on. But when is enough—*enough*?

Social media has amplified this culture of competition. There is even a name for it: FOMO, or fear of missing out. FOMO encapsulates more than just the pangs of envy at what others are doing; it's an ambient mindset of comparing oneself to others on your newsfeed.

A competitive mindset is a habit—and it's one we need to make a conscious effort to break. In Arthur Brooks' *Atlantic* column "How to Build a Life," he once wrote about how we like to keep "score" with others by compiling a checklist of our accomplishments. The person with the most boxes checked wins the "game of life."

We know this is a fallacy. Yet, we can get caught up in this thinking, and it can trap us in a cycle of wanting to outdo others. This is an unhealthy, keeping-up-with-the-Joneses mindset, and it prevents us from becoming our most authentic selves—that is, living our legacies.

David Foster Wallace shared another perspective on these ideas in his 2005 commencement speech at Kenyon College, later published as his book *This Is Water*. To resist the pull of the ego, he spoke of the importance of choosing what we "worship"—whether we're driven by materialistic goals or a desire for greater power or intellect, we are often swayed by unconscious impulses.

Checking your ego, however, forces you to become conscious of these deeply ingrained drives.

Breadcrumb Box:

When I was in college, I went home with my college roommate, Beth, for a holiday. While her parents were missionaries in India in the 1960s, her sister, Ruth, was born with Down Syndrome.

I remember saying to my friend's mom, "You are so good with Ruth and she is lucky to have you both as parents." Beth and her two other siblings are all accomplished and Ruth has lived as independently as possible. Then Beth's mom shared a story.

She told me how some kids in elementary and middle school had been mean at times to her children—bullying them and even throwing rocks at one of them. But Ruth's friends were kind to everyone.

Then she said something I have always remembered and shared with my college students as a life lesson: Bullying and competitive behaviors are learned from an early age from observing others.

To encourage high achievement, traditional schooling can implicitly emphasize negative behaviors: competition can lead to a harshness toward others, even ruthless manipulation. Yet Ruth's school focused on everyday social skills: kindness, acceptance, understanding. People are not born as bullies. The opposite is also true. The ego often prevents us from being nice to everyone.

The Two Sides of the Ego

While we are aware we have an ego, we may not realize that it has two sides. In Jungian psychology, these are known as the light side (positive) and the dark or shadow side (negative). When you don't understand this concept of the ego, it is hard to be the best version of yourself.

Ultimately, the ego wants to protect us. In fact, it is important to have an ego or it would be hard to stand up! A healthy ego—our light side— enables us to have confidence, speak our truth, and do the right things for the right reasons.

When the dark side of the ego takes over, it is trying to protect us. Psychotherapist David Richo, one of the leading authorities on ego development, has an interesting way of describing this.

"It is as if we are walking through life with a dog on one side and a wolf on the other side," he told me.

The more you feed the dog, the more good comes through you. The more you feed the wolf, the more evil or negative potential comes through. There is no way to eliminate either one. Hitler had a dog and Mother Teresa had a wolf.

The wolf side is reflected in behaviors such as arrogance, overly controlling behavior, entitlement, judging, or selfishness. This side brings out our envy, aggression, competitiveness, and jealousy—even if you think you have it under control.

Everyone has the potential to do things that are ethically wrong or hurtful to themselves or others. Most of us deny our shadow. Richo said the more we are triggered or upset by other people's negative behaviors, the more clues we are getting that maybe we have that same inclination in ourselves and are not aware of it. The real danger is denying the shadow. And we can never get rid of it. The shadow is part of being human.

For leaders, this protection often manifests itself in negative behaviors such as defensiveness, micromanaging, envy, and competitiveness. These traits can have a negative impact on your workplace's culture and morale.

Because of this, our ego often interferes with our journey to becoming good people and leaving a positive legacy. Remember Enron, Arthur Anderson, and Theranos. When the ego and shadow take over, entire companies can fall from grace overnight.

Richo described how we can tame the ego by willfully opposing the wolf's control. Make room for others. See others with compassion and curiosity rather than judgment. Be collaborative rather than competitive. Be happy when others succeed. When leaders are cognizant of this, they can be intentional about controlling the ego, and shine light, rather than darkness, onto their organization.

But where do we learn how to control our ego?

Warren Buffett, always tuned into the importance of living a meaningful life, offered one way of thinking about this. When it comes to making wise decisions, he suggested that there was one overarching principle in life: whether people have an Outer Scorecard or an Inner Scorecard.

For an interview in *Inc.*, Buffett explained that an Outer Scorecard measures a person's success based on external validation from other people. An Inner Scorecard measures a person's success against their own value system. Think of it as taking the higher and often longer road to success.

In other words, the ego—which fuels the desires on Buffett's Outer Scorecard—can disrupt the introspection we've been doing to find our purpose. When you define your self-worth in terms of the way that others perceive you, you may not only veer far off course from your own fulfillment, but also create a toxic workplace for others.

So how do we stop the ego from interfering with these processes? In his book *The Infinite Game,* Simon Sinek explains how we are accustomed to approaching life as a finite game, where there are players, set rules, and a clear time to end—a scarcity mindset. As in all sports, there are winners and losers. But in infinite games, players come and go, rules change, and there is no finish line—an abundance mindset. The infinite game is truer to life; there are no winners and losers in business or politics.

Sinek maintains that too many leaders play the infinite game with a finite mindset—meaning that the ego is in control. And it is hard to be a good person when the ego is calling the shots.

Richo also explained to me how it is hard to control the ego by yourself. Because of this, a spiritual practice can be helpful, meaning a regular activity that connects you with a higher power or secular purpose. Such a practice will remind you to direct your energy outward, keep going toward the light—to the side of you that is healthy and good rather than the part that is dark.

A spiritual practice will keep you on track and accountable. Without one, it is easy to take advantage of others or even hurting yourself. Consider the image of a plumb line: the weighted cord that painters and carpenters use to keep their work aligned. A plumb line can also be a metaphor for establishing what is true, straight, or in balance.

We need to assemble a toolbox that will help keep our life in balance. You'll let go of competitiveness. Keep others' needs in mind. Acknowledge when you don't know the answer or need help. Take feedback without getting defensive. Apologize when you've offended someone. Welcome disagreement. You'll notice you are no longer approaching life from the dark side, and that you cast more light than darkness on those you meet.

Breadcrumb Box:

I personally have struggled with the word "authenticity." What if people are authentically bad, which keeps them from being kind? When I interviewed Bill George, executive fellow at Harvard Business School, he explained it this way:

> There's no such thing as an authentically bad person. There must be a reason they are angry or mean. Let's go back and process the crucibles—the things in their life that made them act in these ways. It could have to do with how they were parented, or their financial situation caused them to be this way. There are usually reasons for why people behave the way they do and often they need help processing these crucibles. Maybe you can be the leader who helps them figure this out.

Would You Follow Yourself?

This is a question I ask participants in courses and workshops. It gets their attention. In fact, some students have told me it is a question they can't stop thinking about long after the course is over.

One of my main conclusions in *Leading with Wisdom* is that leadership development is really personal development. It is hard to be a good leader if you aren't a good person.

It is common for people to attend leadership institutes, programs, and seminars to refine their skills. They take courses and read books. Many of these leadership books land on bestseller lists. With all of this preparation, why are there so many bad leaders?

One of the Sages I interviewed for *Leading with Wisdom* was André Delbecq. In the *Journal of Management Inquiry,* Delbecq wrote an article titled "'Evil' Manifested in Destructive Individual Behavior: A Senior Leadership Challenge." He defined the evil individual as someone who "sucks the life juices from the organizational group by unusually destructive behavior, crippling the group in such a way that all positive spirit is lost."

Delbecq wants to believe that most leaders want to be good bosses, but they are often unaware of their blind spots that negatively affect others. While people who demonstrate deeply hurtful behaviors are rare, they do exist, and they create unhealthy environments for others.

I don't think most people wake up in the morning and say, "Today I am going to be a bad leader and a nasty person. I am going to make people's lives miserable by creating a toxic environment." Yet, this is a common motif in our culture: the *Horrible Bosses* films find absurd humor in the emotions that emerge while working for difficult people.

Leadership begins with self-knowledge and insight. It is important to understand one's strengths, but when applied to an extreme, these abilities can become liabilities: perhaps by micromanaging, or creating a psychologically stressful work environment.

Marcus Buckingham and Donald Clifton discuss this in their books *Discover Your Strengths* and *CliftonStrengths*. Not only does this nastiness damage people psychologically and emotionally, but it often increases costs by driving people out of the organization and productivity down.

Similar to Russian Matryoshka dolls, each nested inside of another, we have to dig deep into our core to face our fears and inner demons if we want to continue to grow into our healthiest selves.

Breathe Life into Others

My favorite definition of leadership comes from a seminar I attended facilitated by Peter Senge, author of *The Fifth Discipline* and founder of the Society for Organizational Learning. He asked us to come up with different words for "leader" and people mentioned words like inspiration or aspiration.

Senge reminded us that *spire* comes from the Latin root meaning "breathe." Therefore, he defines leadership as the ability to "breathe life into someone or something."

I have modified this by saying, "Leaders breathe life into people, programs, and projects." Similar to a balloon, you feel bigger when air is blown in. Likewise, toxic leaders make you feel as if you can't breathe freely. You feel like you are choking in their presence. A bad leader pops your balloon!

So how do we keep that balloon intact?

One way to keep the ego in check is to practice humility. In his classic book, *Good to Great: Why Some Companies Make the Leap ... and Others Don't*, Jim Collins defines outstanding leaders as exceedingly humble. They're willing—even eager—to give others praise and credit for a job well done. When projects don't go as planned, they're reflective enough to assign blame on themselves.

If leaders show up to work like selfless team players, they are more likely to be admired by others—and inspire others to lead in the same way. Humble leaders care a great deal about succession planning and generative leadership. They aren't focused on their personal control over their company's destiny; rather, they are focused on leaving it in a strong position for future leaders.

Controlling the Ego Is Necessary—Not Touchy-Feely

Several years ago, I was fortunate enough to meet David L. Bradford, the Eugene O'Kelly II Senior Lecturer Emeritus in Leadership at Stanford University, at a national teaching conference.

As a sign of respect and admiration, the David L. Bradford Outstanding Educator Award is given at this conference. I was honored that he agreed to be one of the Sages I interviewed for *Leading with Wisdom*. Bradford is a special person because he casts a light when he is in the room.

A few years ago, I met up with Bradford at this same conference. When I told him that my son was going to be attending the Graduate School of Business at Stanford (GSB), the first thing he said was, "Make sure he takes the 'touchy-feely' course."

The official course title is "Organizational Behavior 374: Interpersonal Dynamics" and Bradford was instrumental in creating the course. Stanford students and faculty call it the "touchy-feely" course. The GSB has been offering the course for over 50 years to MBA students. It's an elective, but 95 percent of students take it. Based on decades of experience teaching this course and coaching executives, Bradford and co-author Carole Robin published *Connect: Building Exceptional Relationships with Family, Friends, and Colleagues*.

Basically, it's a course on emotional intelligence. Themes covered include open communication, relationship building, self-awareness, and giving and receiving feedback. These are otherwise known as the "soft skills": the interpersonal skills we rely on. The "hard skills" are the quantitative skills where there are data-based, concrete answers, such as finance and accounting.

Interestingly, our educational system is more concerned with preparing people with hard skills to list on a résumé than with teaching students the soft skills. But the soft skills are really the hard skills for people to learn and to practice. As Joan Gallos, an authority on leadership, said to me a few years ago, "The fluff is the stuff"–the soft skills help us become healthy leaders—and people.

Jeremy Hunter, an associate professor at the Peter F. Drucker School of Management, framed it differently. In a personal communication, Hunter told me, "There are the hard skills and then there are the harder skills. There's nothing soft about them."

The word "soft" can feel like it diminishes these skills, but they are truly indispensable. They are integral to our success not only at work, but also as we strive to become our best selves in all aspects of life.

Legacy Thinking

Often leaders are selected for the wrong reasons. We frequently encounter the hero leader, who is popular and placed on a pedestal by followers. They are charismatic, but lack character. They have style, but lack substance. They are highly profiled, but lack integrity. The dark side of this model of leadership is a fear of displaying vulnerability through any perceived imperfection. These insecurities can be masked as excessive pride, a sense of entitlement, arrogance, and difficulty accepting responsibility for mistakes.

But leaders are people, and people make mistakes. Apologizing for one's errors and forgiving others for their imperfections are powerful actions to take.

Thomas Harris' popular 1967 self-help book may have been titled *I'm OK—You're OK*, but I think we should approach others with this philosophy: "I'm not OK—and you're not OK—and *that's OK*." This is a perspective rooted in grace; nobody is perfect, including the people with whom we are working and living.

Admitting mistakes with a sense of grace is a powerful way to lead and to live. People are more likely to want to listen to, follow, and work with others who realize when they are wrong and are strong enough to admit it.

Forgiveness is *not* usually a skill that's highlighted in descriptions of leadership, but it is a skill needed for all of our relationships. It is also a skill that needs to be practiced. Every day, we encounter opportunities to learn to forgive, each of which can be a breadcrumb worth remembering.

When we practice forgiveness, it stops the dark side from taking over and dominating our thoughts and behaviors. Once again, it is a skill that turns our focus outward.

From Nobody to Somebody

While many of the concepts that help us become better leaders and better people may be common sense, often they are not common practice. This is why it's important to consciously cultivate them.

Along those lines, we need to understand that all of this is a process. We won't suddenly transform into the *perfect* leader or person—but perhaps perfection isn't what we should strive to attain. Instead, if we discover our strengths, remain vigilant of our dark sides, and stay aware of the breadcrumbs we scatter through our decisions and behavior, then we will help create an environment where people want to work...and live a life worth remembering.

Back to Rick Moody. While he told me that the teachings of Ram Dass popularized the idea of "becoming a nobody," the term should really be credited to Emily Dickinson. While she was anonymous and reclusive while alive, Dickinson's work was discovered and celebrated after her death.

Moody told me how it is harder to be a nobody if you are famous. We observe many celebrities and athletes struggling to let go and move on to what's next in life. According to Moody, we should not let the ego rule us, regardless of age—age should be irrelevant.

This often involves tuning out our surroundings, especially when our society measures success based on activity and productivity. It's far too tempting to equate our net worth with our self-worth.

One of the most selfless leaders I know is Janette Larkin, former president and publisher of Business Publications Corporation, Inc. She demonstrated to me how to let go from the inside out. I was amazed at how she was able to "let go" of this identity in her life and work; she did not even want a retirement party.

When I asked Larkin how she was able to shed her ego in order to move on, this was her response:

> When you are in community journalism, civic and community involvement is part of the position. Organizations seek you out and want you to be on their boards. The position vaults you into the world. Community service is a time commitment that is expected with the position.
>
> I was aware that my position gave me opportunities that I would not have had just because of me. It wasn't all about me and I knew this. And I knew when I left the position, I would lose the privilege of people seeking me out—that my influence would be less because it accompanies the position.

Larkin's leadership philosophy stems from her innate desire to help others who need a leg up. Her goal is to boost the efforts of her colleagues every day, and, to paraphrase the advice of leadership guru John Maxwell, be a prime role model of a "lifter" in the workplace.

"I got excited about stepping out of the organization to let others step up," remembered Larkin:

> I didn't want to block opportunities for others. One of the things I enjoy is mentoring others to get them ready to step up. My motivation was always to help others. This seemed natural to me, which helps to keep the ego in check.

As the saying goes: Your ego is not your amigo.

Life is about choices. With every moment, we can decide to be a somebody or a nobody. In 2021, I gave a virtual talk with TEDxBergenCommunityCollege titled "Becoming a Nobody." My conclusion was "choosing to be a nobody is in reality choosing to be somebody special."

Breadcrumb Box:

When I interviewed Carol Orsborn, author of *The Making of an Old Soul: Aging as the Fulfillment of Life's Promise*, she had an interesting perspective on legacy. Orsborn has been writing about adult development for decades. She shared this story:

> Years ago, I was studying to earn a brown belt in karate. When it was time for the test, I was extremely nervous. I've always remembered what my teacher said to me. "Who shows up on the day of the test is the person you've become and that is your ordinary self. Don't strive to be extraordinary. Be who you've become."
>
> For me, legacy means living life out of love every day. Be kind to the person getting on the bus. Do something for someone when they don't expect it... I have moved beyond caring about being remembered. I believe in what Ram Dass said about becoming a nobody. He said, "You'll never be enlightened if you care about being a somebody."
>
> COVID was a good reminder that most of us wear masks when we try to measure up to society's expectations. But Jung said the purpose of life is to become more conscious. Similar to fish, we don't see the water in which we're swimming. But I am hopeful because of the spiritual awakening that happened during the pandemic.

Breadcrumb Ingredients for Becoming a Nobody

Make Me Feel Important:

Have you been around someone who made you feel *unimportant?* One way to keep your ego in check is to focus on others. Imagine everyone you see has a sign hanging around their neck that says: MAKE ME FEEL IMPOR-TANT. Think about what makes you feel important: recognition, feedback, acknowledgment of some kind, being asked questions. So, see what happens when you look outward toward someone else. Pay attention to how the mental image of this sign changes your perspective about others.

Serve:

When feeling lonely, focus on how to serve others. This shifts the focus from ourselves to someone else. Serving others reminds us of our talents and the value we can offer others. What could you do for someone else right now? Invite someone to have a conversation. Take a meal to an ill person. Run errands for a neighbor who can't drive. These are all tiny breadcrumbs that are externally focused.

To Say or Do, or Not:

Years ago, our pastor gave a sermon that stayed with me. It has kept me out of trouble and has helped keep my ego in check. He recommended asking yourself these three questions before you say or do anything:

*   Is it true?
*   Is it kind?
*   Is it necessary?

If you can't say "yes," then you should not say it or do it.

Each question can be a breadcrumb that guides our choices, helping us keep the dark side of our ego in check.

Bibliography

Ander, S. (Director). (2014). *Horrible Bosses 2.* [Film]. Benderspink.

Bradford, D. & Robin, C. (2021). *Connect: Building exceptional relationships with family, friends, and colleagues.* New York: Currency.

Brooks, A. C. (January 21, 2021). "Stop keeping score." *The Atlantic.* https://www.theatlantic.com/family/archive/2021/01/checklist-achievements-happiness-boxes/617756/

Buckingham, M. & Clifton, D. O. (2001). *Discover your strengths.* New York: The Free Press.

Catto, J. (Director). (2020). *Becoming Nobody*. Love Serve Remember Films, with Google Empathy Lab.

Collins, J. (2001). *Good to great: Why some companies make the leap … and others don't*. New York: HarperCollins Publishers, Inc.

Delbecq A. L. (2001). "'Evil' manifested in destructive individual behavior: A senior leadership challenge." *Journal of Management Inquiry*, 10(3), 221–226.

Ehrmann, M. (1995). "Desiderata." In *Desiderata: A poem for a way of life*. Crown (Original work published 1920). https://en.wikipedia.org/wiki/Desiderata

Frankl, V. E. (2006). *Man's search for meaning*. Boston, MA: Beacon Press.

Freed, J. E. (2013). *Leading with wisdom: Sage advice from 100 experts*. Alexandria: ATD.

Freed, J. E. (October 29, 2021). "Becoming a Nobody." TEDxBergenCommunity College.

Gee, K. (May 1, 2019). "Stanford pushes executives to get 'touchy-feely'." *The Wall Street Journal*. https://www.wsj.com/articles/stanford-pushes-executives-to-get-touchy-feely-11556719200

Gordon, S. (Director). (2011). *Horrible Bosses*. [Film]. New Line Cinema.

Harris, T. A. (1967). *I'm OK—You're OK: A practical guide to transactional analysis*. New York: Harper & Row.

Maruca, R. F. & Galford, R. M. (2006). *Your leadership legacy: Why looking toward the future will make you a better leader today*. Boston, MA: Harvard Business School Press.

Moody, H. R. & Carroll, D. (1998). *The five stages of the soul. Charting the spiritual passages that shape our lives*. Hamburg: Anchor.

Orsborn, C. (2021). The making of an old soul: Aging as the fulfillment of life's promise. Bucklin, MO: White River Press.

Schwantes, M. (April 2020). "Warren Buffett has a simple test for living your best life. Here's how it works." *Inc*. https://www.inc.com/marcel-schwantes/warren-buffetts-simple-test-for-living-your-best-life.html

Senge, P. M. (2006). *The fifth discipline: The art & practice of the learning organization*. New York: Currency.

Sinek, S. (2019). *The infinite game*. New York: Portfolio/Penguin.

Wallace, D. F. (2009). *This is water: Some thoughts, delivered on a significant occasion, about living a compassionate life*. New York: Little, Brown and Company.

Chapter 5

Death through a Different Lens

Call me Dr. Death.

At least, my students do…

Learning about death, dying, grief, and grieving has changed my life. I think about death all of the time. I plan and revise my funeral the way other people plan weddings or parties.

I relate to Maude's love of going to funerals in the classic movie *Harold and Maude*. There is so much to be learned about someone, and about life, by what others share in remembrance.

I don't think about death in a way that is depressing or ghoulish, though. Quite the opposite. The way that I think about death has made me a better friend and, I think, a better person. Of all the concepts in this book, the ones contained in this chapter have had the greatest impact on my life.

In fact, these ideas were the focus of my 2021 TEDxDesMoines talk titled "Embracing Death: Life Through a Different Lens" I explained how I teach people to accept that we all have 24 hours in a day, but we don't know when our days will end. If we are able to envision how we want to be remembered, then we don't have to wait to start living our lives that way. And the earlier we understand this concept, the better.

Breadcrumb Legacy explains how to leave the legacy you desire one "crumb" at a time. When we are aware of the trail we are leaving behind, we can be more intentional with everything we say and do. This is our path toward becoming a good person, and this involves embracing the fact that we will die.

The Latin phrase *memento mori* means "remember your death." By thinking intentionally about death, we will have a greater appreciation for the present and an ability to focus more fully on the future: the defining philosophies of *Breadcrumb Legacy*. Embracing death in this way can help us see our lives through a different lens.

Finding Freedom in Life

After working with terminally ill patients for years, Bonnie Ware often heard her patients express regrets as they reflected on their lives. So she wrote the popular book *The Top Five Regrets of the Dying*.

DOI: 10.4324/9781003310211-5

Ware believes the book resonates with people as a reminder that we "only have a limited time to live the life we choose ourselves." More importantly, she believes it "gives people permission to change direction. That's what it triggers—it's a wake-up call, and gives them permission to change tack."

We need to know that someday, perhaps sooner rather than later, we're going to die, and we have to be OK with that. When we're aware of our impending death without fearing it, we become paradoxically freer to live.

It is commonly said the two things people fear the most are death and public speaking. This may not be accurate—people do not fear death, they fear dying—but death is certainly a taboo subject in our culture. Most of us don't like to think about death and we especially don't like to talk about it.

There is evidence that more and more people are hungry to bring this topic out into the open. Recent nonfiction accounts of the quality of life as it nears its end have been *New York Times* bestsellers, including Atul Gawande's *Being Mortal* and Paul Kalanithi's *When Breath Becomes Air*. Joan Didion's *The Year of Magical Thinking*, which delves into Didion's grief for her husband John Gregory Dunne, was made into a Broadway play.

People are also eager to discuss death informally. In 2010, Pulitzer Prize–winning writer Ellen Goodman and a group of colleagues got together to share stories of "good deaths" and "hard deaths" among their families and friends. This conversation was the stimulus for creating The Conversation Project, a group that helps society shift toward openly discussing death.

In 2011, Jon Underwood founded the Death Cafe movement in the UK. Rather than a grief support group or counseling session, Death Cafes are spaces that welcome open-ended philosophical conversations. Underwood hoped to encourage people to broach this difficult topic with a view toward making the most of their limited time. Inspired by the ideas of Swiss sociologist Bernard Crettaz, Underwood opened the first Death Cafe in his kitchen in East London. Now, there are similar "cafes" in countries all over the world.

There is a broader movement to change the conversation around death. The End in Mind Project is a community engagement project that seeks to help people live with intention, purpose, and meaning—to live more and fear less.

Rachael Freed of Life Legacies echoed the importance of speaking openly about death. She advises doing so through legacy letters and ethical wills. The practice of writing legacy letters becomes even more important as families disperse across the country, and even the world. When we are physically separated, it becomes more difficult to pass on what matters most to us.

An ethical will is a similar concept. It takes the form of a "last letter home" that a member of the military might write: as if you may not make it back home, and have one final chance to share yourself with your family. It can contain your wishes, thoughts, feelings, memories, life lessons—anything that you hold dear.

"Legacy letters give us permission to write about our values and what's important to us," Freed explained. "We don't have to be old or retired to write legacy letters and to have our affairs in order."

Often, life landmarks move us to express ourselves more deeply to others: graduations, relocations, weddings, and funerals, among others. Like legacy letters, an ethical will can be written at any age, and updated whenever the spirit moves us to do so.

It can be a love letter to your family and friends, or even help you repair relationships by making amends. Barry Baines and Tracie Ward, the founders of the Minneapolis-based group LivingWisely, call an ethical will the "voice of the heart."

Breadcrumb Box:

Sara Davidson, journalist and author of the seminal book *Loose Change*, related these stories to me:

> Reb Zalman prepared for his dying and death for decades. He had a detailed dress rehearsal when his body was breaking down. He believed there was something after—"something continues" he would say. I am a skeptic and not so sure.
>
> He staged his death. He was excited about having his body blessed as we do in the Jewish faith. He always followed his inner knowings better than anyone I have known. He was a Holocaust survivor so death was a reality for him. He was aware that he could die at any moment. He was always looking forward and didn't look in the rearview mirror very often.
>
> About Ram Dass. I was lucky to know both men. I was at the Celebration of Life for Ram Dass. I wrote a book titled: *Ram Dass Has a Son* (Kindle). He lived with fierce grace and there is a documentary about him with that same title. His mantra was: Love everyone, feed everyone, serve everyone, and tell the truth. He lived his life by these principles.

The Need for Empathy and Compassion

In The Great Recession of 2008, Americans lost millions of jobs, hundreds of companies closed, and the banking system nearly collapsed. The COVID-19 pandemic was even more devastating: to date, over 1 million deaths in the United States, and over 200,000 small businesses shuttered.

When companies and industries disappear—and the jobs, relationships, and familiar ways of life with them—our human psyche naturally drives us to grieve for these losses even if we don't admit it.

According to the Grief Recovery Institute, hidden grief costs U.S. companies more than 100 billion dollars in lost productivity. The Institute studies the costs associated with multiple losses such as:

* Death of a loved one
* Divorce
* Family crisis
* Financial loss
* Death of extended family, colleagues, and friends
* Major lifestyle alterations
* Pet loss

Few, if any, business and MBA programs require courses on loss, death, or grief as part of their curriculum. Compassion and empathy are usually considered to be "soft skills." These interpersonal skills may not be given the attention needed in unprecedented times.

But every reaction we have, or lack thereof, to a loss—an ending—is a breadcrumb. People will remember how you made them feel by the things you said or did not say, or by how you acted. Learning to approach times of mourning with compassion and empathy is critical.

Interestingly, many positive life events, such as promotions and weddings, also entail a sense of loss. This is because significant change often triggers a grieving process for the way life used to be.

Without grief training and education, it is easy for leaders to do and say the wrong thing. Organizational policies indicate that grief should be quantified, or compartmentalized into a culturally accepted window of time. For example, companies create arbitrary human resource policies that state how many days away from the office are allowed for major losses—the death of a spouse or family member.

Yet, work is a place where a majority of our lives are spent. Few leaders have the training to equip them to deal with loss and workplace grief, not to mention the other life events that manifest grief responses. But it's essential to learn these skills in order to be an effective and compassionate leader.

To help employees thrive, leaders must create workplaces that encourage healing and minimize pain, especially in times of grief. With this understanding, their breadcrumb trail will be one that others will remember.

Breadcrumb Box:

Ruth Graham wrote a spring 2021 *New York Times* article about Sister Aletheia, a nun who is passionate about the value of embracing death. Her work has been integrated into religious education curricula at Catholic parishes.

The foundation of her philosophy is the Latin phrase memento mori: "remember your death." The concept is to intentionally think about your own death every day, as a means of appreciating the present and focusing on the future.

Sister Aletheia wrote in her devotional: "Remembering death keeps us awake, focused, and ready for whatever might happen—both the excruciatingly difficult and the breathtakingly beautiful." When Sister Aletheia translates it, she asks: "Where am I headed, where do I want to end up?"

Understanding Coping Mechanisms

When I developed my leadership course, I was completing training to be a Certified Sage-ing Leader through Sage-ing© International. One of the main components of becoming a Sage is befriending death, even by scripting our own death. This helps to overcome fear and enables us to have more courage to take risks.

If you don't understand your own coping mechanisms, helping others through the grieving process is difficult, if not impossible. One of the assignments I give to undergraduate students between the ages of 20 and 22 (and then to graduate students with an average age of 35) is to write their own eulogy—which is different from an obituary.

When I started giving this assignment in 2008, obituaries and eulogies served divergent purposes. Obituaries tend to focus on facts—what a person has done (doing). Eulogies tend to focus on character—what the person was like (being). During the last decade, I've noticed more overlap: obituaries are sounding more like eulogies, and some people are even writing their own.

Early in the course, I tell students that this eulogy will be one of their mandatory assignments, written to share aloud at the semester's end. But I never explain the purpose of the exercise. Most of the students react with confusion, and several have expressed how they dreaded it, unable to see the point at first.

This is why I schedule the assignment for the end of the course, and give them fair warning in advance. It takes time to create a sacred and safe space where students feel comfortable sharing something so personal.

Midway through the course, I share examples of actual eulogies I've collected through the years. For example, I have students watch Tim

Russert's memorial service. Russert was a journalist and long-time moderator of NBC's *Meet the Press* who died suddenly in 2008. The speakers at the service are noted journalists who are recognized for their way with words, and they share moving and thoughtful memories.

There were several days of television coverage in remembrance of Tim Russert, which some felt was too much. But Peggy Noonan in the *Wall Street Journal* indicated she thought it was justified because these were life lessons from a life well-lived. Noonan pointed out how young adults need role models such as Russert to emulate.

There are no rules for the Eulogy Assignment. Students can write it in first or third person, as if they lived to be 85 or died tomorrow. No right or wrong; not graded, just mandatory. We laugh, we cry. Some are serious, funny. Some are written as poetry, put to music, or follow a theme (such as shoes, in one creative and memorable example).

This assignment is also an exercise in compassion and empathy. One poignant example is when a big football player, over 6 feet tall and about 300 pounds, got emotional when he stood up to share. Since he had trouble continuing, a female student asked if she could read his eulogy for him. You could hear a pin drop. It was a perfect demonstration of compassion, empathy, and the willingness to be vulnerable.

When I talk about this course at academic conferences, people are surprised I'm facilitating this exercise with students in their early 20s. But student feedback indicates that participants find it to be the most meaningful part of the course.

By the time we share these eulogies, we've done enough work to create the right environment. The students are able to connect all of the dots to understand the purpose of the exercise: *If this is how you want to be remembered, start living your life like that now.*

And the earlier they understand this, the better.

Life Is a Series of Transitions

For my book, *Leading with Wisdom*, I interviewed more than 100 Sages—people at the peak of their careers—and framed the book around the themes and insights that emerged.

My driving question to them was, *How can I best prepare people to be the kinds of leaders needed in these uncertain times?* Since the book was published in 2013, the times have only become more uncertain.

I realize now that I was learning about how to become a good person through breadcrumbs of wisdom. When I would learn new ideas and practices suggested by the Sages, I would do them myself. Therefore, I refer to this book as my "eat, pray, love" book of leadership.

One of the biggest "ahas" in my research was that leaders need to understand death, dying, and grieving. They explained that in addition to the death of people and pets, industries and companies are dying, and positions are disappearing. More frequently than we might assume, people are grieving personal and professional losses.

During my leadership research, I was fortunate to interview William Bridges twice. Bridges, the author of several books on how to navigate transitions in life and work, developed a Transition Framework that is used by leaders in organizations and communities to help make deep change.

Bridges differentiates between "change" and "transition." Change tends to be an external event that happens to us, while transition is an internal process. He suggests that some people "make changes so they won't have to make transitions." It is important to understand both processes.

Life is a series of transitions, and a transition is a response to change. They say the only constant is change. After the daily changes and uncertainty of the COVID-19 pandemic, we know this statement could not be truer.

Some changes are personal, and some changes are widespread, affecting many people. We get married or divorced. We have children and they leave for college—sometimes they return home. We get promoted—we lose jobs. We move to another neighborhood—our parents move back to town. Regardless of the change, all changes force us to go through a process of psychological and emotional adjustment: a transition.

With every change comes a "death": an ending. The death could be a "big D" (a significant ending) or a "little d" (a minor change). But something must end before something new can begin. All endings involve grief and loss to varying degrees.

With this in mind, we need to "let go" of the way things used to be and prepare ourselves to accept the way things are. (Reflect on what we learned about dropping our tools: it is important to confront reality and, if necessary, abandon habits that no longer serve us.)

When we don't let go, we feel stressed, overworked, depleted, and exhausted. And the costs of stress and distress are high for individuals and organizations.

Contrary to our typical assumptions, we don't resist the external process of change. Rather, we resist the inner and emotional workings of transition. We resist turning away from the way life was, or the way we thought it was. We resist taking on a new identity or embracing the new situation.

In Bridges' framework, a transition consists of three stages:

1. **Endings:** which often result in sadness, anger, or remorse. We start with Endings because we can't move ahead without leaving something else behind. While learning to let go, we need to realize that people and organizations must grieve for what was lost.

2. **The Neutral Zone:** which results in fear and confusion. It is not so much that we are afraid of change or so in love with the old ways, but we often find ourselves somewhere in between. We feel unsteady, like being caught between trapezes—dangling in the neutral zone.
3. **New Beginnings:** which inspire a mix of confidence over what has been gained, anxiety about what has been lost, and a dose of worry about slipping back into old habits.

Interestingly, we don't mind endings or new beginnings as much as we dread the Neutral Zone. This is why we go from one bad job to another, one bad relationship to another. We resist spending time in the Neutral Zone to process, reflect, and learn about why it ended or why the change took place. Bridges says we can't begin something new until something else ends. Each ending is like a mini-death.

In Bruce Feiler's book *Life Is in the Transitions: Mastering Change at Any Age,* he observes that Bridges' framework characterizes life as a *linear* experience. We are trained to expect a straightforward progression in our lives, moving easily through school, jobs, marriage, and life. Hopefully a linear line of moving up!

But Feiler adds that this linear life is dead. It is being replaced by the nonlinear life, consisting of many more disruptions and transitions.

Feiler defines disruptors as "everyday events that reshape our lives." He estimates that the average adult faces 30–40 disruptors in their lives, and that they appear every 12–18 months.

We often think of these events negatively, supposedly as evidence that life is not going as we planned. But these small shifts that affect daily life can also be positive.

Sometimes they dramatically alter the direction of your life—Feiler calls these significant transitions "lifequakes." Feiler refers to the Neutral Zone as the Messy Middle because of how we can feel lost, confused, and frustrated.

But regardless of what happens, it's important to view these transitions as an unavoidable part of life: accept the present and drop your tools.

When we resist transition, the external change usually goes poorly. Productivity is often lower, and costs are higher. Feelings of apathy and disengagement can fester. The workplace feels dehumanized when people are treated as disposable commodities—assets to depreciate instead of appreciate.

Instead, leaders need to provide the resources, time, and energy to support people through various life changes. For this to work, it is critically important for people to understand *why* the change is taking place. This is a psychological process, making the internal experience of transition much smoother.

Accepting transition will allow you to treat others with a greater degree of empathy, especially people who may not be handling change well. As a leader, you can help people manage endings successfully, navigate the

Neutral Zone, and support new beginnings. It is time to change how you think about change.

Breadcrumb Box:

Rob Salafia, CEO of Protagonist Consulting Group, reflected on these ideas during our conversation:

Death is not an ending. How can you possibly live life to its fullest if life is ending? Similar to martial arts, we have to "punch through the board." I say "no" to retirement because that is an end. We have to become masters of transitions. What am I in the process of becoming?

How This Work Changed My Life

So my students call me Dr. Death, a nickname I earned because I talk about death and grief a lot—probably too much. Some of this goes back to the time when I studied and then taught college courses in Mexico.

Since studying in Yucatan in college, Mexico and its culture have been an important part of my life. The photographs, decorations, and memories in my home would show you its impact on my life. In fact, I co-authored a book of essays and photographs with my colleague George Ann Huck titled *Women of Yucatan: Thirty Who Dare to Change Their World*.

One custom I find intriguing and meaningful is the annual Latin American celebration, Día de Muertos: Day of the Dead. On this day, families gather to honor loved ones who have died, as they believe their souls return to visit the living in homes, businesses, and cemeteries. It's a festive event, full of music and life.

It is common to create altars with photographs of the person being remembered, surrounded by food, flowers, mementos, and favorite items of the deceased. Anything goes, if you have seen one of these altars. Through these remembrances, the Latin American cultures that observe this holiday maintain a more positive attitude toward death. The end of life is an occasion to celebrate their loved ones' legacy.

This work has changed how I lead my life. It has become my practice to write personal notes to people whose stories of loss move me. These people may be local or national, but often they are people I don't know and they don't know me. If I can't stop thinking about someone's story, I write a note and often include a memorial gift. I also have a small collection of the most thoughtful thank-you notes I've received in response.

This grief work has also encouraged me to spark conversations that others may be afraid to have. At our church, one of our long-time members announced she was diagnosed with pancreatic cancer, and she was open about not having long to live. I called her daughter to express sympathy.

During our conversation, I suggested she consider having a celebration of life now while her mom can enjoy it. It could take on any tone and style that her mom would want—if she would want this. "We could serve wine!" she said. "Mom would like that."

I could tell she had never thought of having a service for her mom that she could enjoy while she is still alive. Honestly, I was inspired to suggest this because of one of my favorite books, *Tuesdays with Morrie*. Morrie, who has ALS and knows the end is near, has a celebration of life with his family and friends while he is alive to enjoy it. Breadcrumb inspiration can come from anywhere, if you are open to it.

A good friend of mine, I'll call her Sally, was in an experimental treatment program for cancer that had metastasized. She knew her time was limited. In fact, her daughter moved her wedding up six months in the hopes that Sally could attend.

Sally asked me what I was working on and I shared my concept of *Breadcrumb Legacy* with her. I described legacy letters and the value of sharing right now what is most important to her. I explained that it was easier to talk about than to do. "You are so brave and willing to be vulnerable," Sally said.

As a hospice volunteer who goes into homes and sits with patients, I have done a lot of grief work. These comments from friends also reflect the grief work I have done independently so I can leave a trail of meaning that matters to me. In fact, Vanda Marlow, is a long-time volunteer with San Francisco's renowned Zen Hospice Project.

Marlow believes that "instead of having national service, we should have national hospice service. If you send 18-, 19-, and 20-year-olds to sit bedside with people at the end of life, it totally would shape how they live their lives." At the end of life, most people reflect on their life and want to share their wisdom, regrets, and lessons learned.

A reappraisal of our priorities can help us create what Ron Pevny, founder and director of the Center for Conscious Eldering, calls a "holistic bucket list." When I interviewed him on my podcast, Pevny told me that we should seek fulfillment in five areas: learning, play, community, relationships, and spirituality.

What if we wrote a bucket list for each of those aspects of life—a list of actions we want to take to feel more fulfilled? Pevny recommended listening to our heart to create a vision, and taking steps toward it.

Similar to Tinker Bell sprinkling pixie dust, you need to be aware of the breadcrumbs you are scattering on a daily basis. If you only had five years left to live, how would your breadcrumbs change? What trail of meaning are you leaving behind? The goal is to align this path with the way you'd like to be remembered.

Breadcrumb Box:

Several years ago, I asked my college roommate and dear friend, Beth, if she would be one of the people who eulogized me at my funeral. She and I have a long history and she knows me so well.

So for my 50th birthday, she wrote my eulogy as she would deliver it at that point in time and gave it to me as my gift. I loved it. And I actually shared parts of it with students over the years as an example since they were going to write their own eulogy.

Beth said she had worked on it at some of her daughter's volleyball games and people wondered what she was working on. While Beth knew it was a perfect gift for me, she found it hard to explain to others.

Now I would advise her to say, "This is part of my Breadcrumb Legacy that I am giving to my friend as part of her Breadcrumb Legacy."

Breadcrumb Ingredients for Embracing Death

Write Your Own Eulogy:

What would you want people to say about you at your funeral? This can be written in the first or third person. There is no right or wrong. It often helps to talk with people who know you well to get their perspective. It is important to think about how you want to be remembered.

Now, Condense Your Own Eulogy:

Write down how you'd want to be remembered in 280 characters or less so it is tweetable. Again, there is no right or wrong way to go about this. This will help you zero in on the breadcrumbs of your legacy that matter most.

Create Rituals and Ceremonies:

Create a ritual or conduct a ceremony to mark the end of a career, a marriage, a friendship, a job or career. The goal is to create a spirit of intention, presence, and gratitude for what once was. These meaningful activities provide lasting memories that help us to let go; as we find healthy ways to move on with our lives, we will help others do the same.

Hospice Volunteer Training:

One way to become comfortable with death, dying, and grieving is to be trained as a hospice volunteer. Contact one of your local hospice organizations and register for their training. This training is excellent for the purpose of personal growth and development even if you don't want to volunteer. It helps you become a better person and friend to those who need your support both in the workplace and outside of work.

Bibliography

Ashby, H. (Director). (1971). *Harold and Maude*. [Film]. Mildred Lewis and Colin Higgins Productions.

Bridges, W. (2001). *The way of transition: Embracing life's most difficult moments*. Cambridge: Da Capo Press.

Davidson, S. (1997). *Loose change: Three women of the sixties*. Berkeley: University of California Press.

Didion, J. (2007). *The year of magical thinking*. New York: Vintage Books.

Feiler, B. (2020). *Life is in the transitions: Mastering change at any age*. New York: Penguin Press.

Freed, J. E. (2013). *Leading with wisdom: Sage advice from 100 experts*. Alexandria: ATD.

Freed, J. E. (May 11, 2021). "Embracing death: Life through a different lens." *TEDxDesMoines*.

Gawande, A. (2017) *Being mortal: Medicine and what matters in the end*. New York: Metropolitan Books.

Graham, R. (May 14, 2021). "Meet the nun who wants you to remember you will die." *The New York Times*. https://www.nytimes.com/2021/05/14/us/memento-mori-nun.html?smid=url-share

Huck, G.A. & Freed, J. E. (2010). *Women of Yucatan: Thirty who dare to change their world*. Jefferson, NC: McFarland & Company.

Kalanithi, P. & Verghese, A. (2016). *When breath becomes air*. New York: Random House.

Moeller, S. (2017) "Grief in the workplace." *The Grief Recovery Institute*. https://www.griefrecoverymethod.com/blog/2017/07/grief-workpla

Noonan, P. (June 20, 2008). "A life's lesson." *The Wall Street Journal*. https://www.wsj.com/articles/SB121390975307189781

Ware, B. (2019). *The top five regrets of the dying: A life transformed by the dearly departed*. Carlsbad, CA: Hay House.

Chapter 6

Who'll Help You Move the Couch?

My husband asked me to help him move the couch.

Now, our couch is sizable. It can fit all three of our grown sons, and it's heavy, too. Since our adult sons live elsewhere, I asked my husband, "Can't you call a friend to help?"

He said he did not want to bother anyone. *Bother,* I thought. *It's not a bother. That's what friends are for.*

I started to think of all of the friends I could call if my husband weren't around. After a moment, I told him, "You need to make more friends."

Every relationship is a breadcrumb that adds to or takes away meaning from our life. Healthy relationships help us survive and thrive. Toxic relationships can literally make us ill.

Loneliness Is Killing Us

The COVID-19 pandemic and required social distancing made us realize how interdependent we are on a global scale. Our social isolation made it clear that we often take relationships for granted.

Yet, we live in an individualistic society and most of us do not like to ask for help. Even in times of loss and grief, we feel as if we have to go it alone.

For these reasons, Robert Putnam's book *Bowling Alone: The Collapse and Revival of American Community* may be more relevant now than when it was written in 2000. He describes how people used to join the PTA, bowling leagues, Masons, Shriners, and the like for a sense of community.

Participation in these organizations has decreased, and now many people feel they are "bowling alone." Social media has made it easier to connect with people we know and don't know—but this is no substitute for real-world interaction. Real face time is better than Apple's FaceTime! More than 40 percent of adults in America report feeling lonely, and research has found that the number of Americans with "no friends" has tripled since 1985.

When we are younger, it is easier to form friendships through organic situations. Joseph Coughlin, who leads the Massachusetts Institute of Technology AgeLab, says that most friendships tend to be "front-end

DOI: 10.4324/9781003310211-6

loaded" through chance encounters that happen on our life journey; for instance, daycare, school, sports, college, work, and community and faith-based activities. All of these settings are conducive to fostering friendships, but they are most common in the earliest phases of our lives.

If we don't continue to form lasting bonds, our social capital—our circle of friends—decreases. Some of the shrinkage is natural as people retire, move, or die. Other relationships just don't last through the cycles of life. Some of the people with whom we left breadcrumbs over the years are no longer there.

Vivek Murthy, the 19th U.S. Surgeon General, has been sounding the alarm about loneliness for years. Murthy's book *Together: The Healing Power of Human Connection in a Sometimes Lonely World* stresses that social isolation is a more serious health problem than opiates, and can shorten our lifespan just as dramatically as "smoking 15 cigarettes a day."

We are social creatures and we need each other. Connection was a means of life-or-death survival for POWs in Vietnam. There is a first-person account written by John McCain, the U.S. senator and former presidential candidate, about the five years in captivity as a POW in North Vietnam.

After he was released, he described how he managed to survive. To keep his mind busy, he devised a way of tapping on the wall to send messages to other prisoners. The simple act of pressing his ear to the wall and listening for those patterns kept him alive.

Groups such as Alcoholics Anonymous and Weight Watchers have shown us the vital importance of collective support. There is also the classic Harvard longitudinal study on cultivating meaningful bonds between men, which concluded: "Close relationships...protect people from life's discontents, help to delay mental and physical decline, and are better predictors of long and happy lives than social class, IQ, or even genes."

Connection can be protection. These waves of isolation may be powerful and we can fight them through breadcrumbs: by thinking more deliberately about how we can support others and how others can support us.

Breadcrumb Box:

When I interviewed Todd Cherches, author of *VisuaLeadership: Leveraging the Power of Visual Thinking in Leadership and Life,* he said the concept of breadcrumbs resonated with him.

> I was a Dale Carnegie trainer and the principles are timeless. They are based on developing leadership skills and they don't go out of style. Each of these could be breadcrumbs: use peoples' names and remember their names—so important. Try to make the other person smile and feel important. Don't try to be the smartest person in the room—give credit to others. And remember to smile.

How Can I Support You?

If people are lonely at home, they are most likely also lonely at work.

I remind people that leadership is not a title or position: it is a relationship. So effective leaders know their job requires building relationships of trust. It is hard to trust someone you don't know.

When leaders understand that their main role is to connect people by building community, then the questions they should be asking are: *What do you need from me? How can I support you?* Leaders need to keep their ears open to what people need.

While I was conducting a "lunch and learn" on why leaders need to cultivate a healthy culture, a young woman in the corporate group left the room. Since the event took place during the lunch hour and it is common for people to respond to a call or email, I didn't take offense to her leaving.

My client informed me later that I had hit a "nerve" with the topic of community, and for this employee it rang true. She revealed that this person was extremely lonely and this discussion was eye-opening. But the employee also considered this revelation a gift. As the team leader, the employee was now going to be more aware and would invest more energy in cultivating trust within her team.

According to Arthur Brooks' book *Strength By Strength: Finding Success, Happiness, and Deep Purpose in the Second Half of Life*, we often find *deal* friends rather than *real* friends at work. Deal friends are strategic and transactional: they may bring you closer to professional success, but you may not have much in common with them. On the other hand, there are real friends, where a bond arises from genuine connection and mutual admiration. But real friends are the bedrock of social wellness—and a healthy workplace.

Leaders need to invest effort in building communities. During the COVID-19 pandemic, technology became our new best friend for connecting. All meetings went virtual regardless of the number of people—from 2 people to more than 100. A friend of mine had a Zoom session for Easter with her 109 cousins!

These programs were a silver lining during the crisis. But a technological tool can't replace interpersonal skills.

There is a difference between being alone and feeling lonely. When I interviewed *Leadership Challenge* author Jim Kouzes, he explained how emotional intelligence has been around for a long time, but relationship skills are getting renewed attention after the pandemic. "We need to find ways to create more cooperation, collaboration, empathy, compassion, agility, learning, DEIJ [diversity, equity, inclusion, and justice], and all of the skills associated with relationships," he told me.

Crumb by crumb, a Breadcrumb Legacy can transform these skills into everyday practice.

Breadcrumb Box:

Tami Simon is the founder of Sounds True, a multi-media publisher dedicated to disseminating spiritual wisdom. When I asked
her about legacy, she said,

> Legacy is like creating a wake behind a boat. I try to get up
> every morning with this question: "What am I called to do?"
> Then I need to listen. I want to give my gifts and "leave it all on
> the court every day." I want to empty out and serve.

In order to build relationships, Simon does the right things: she lis-
tens, and is passionate about giving and receiving feedback. She also
wants what is best for her employees.

> I want people to grow. I would not want them to suffer because
> of me and my leadership practices. I have created a safe and posi-
> tive environment so the unspoken can be spoken. We even give a
> courageous feedback award for people who speak truth to power.

How to Build Relationships

Follow the magic ratio 5:1. John Gottman is an expert on relationships,
particularly romantic and marital relationships. Based on decades of research, Gottman can predict if couples will divorce with 90 percent ac-
curacy. According to the Gottman Institute website, "For every negative
interaction during conflict, a stable and happy marriage has five (or more)
positive interactions."

If this is true for romantic relationships, it makes sense that this type
of balance would also apply to platonic relationships. Small breadcrumbs
of kindness can help build healthy and positive relationships, but the 5:1
ratio also reminds us of the damage a single negative breadcrumb can do.
A wrong look, a thoughtless tone of voice. When we don't think about the
other person, it can take time and effort to heal hurt feelings.

Instead, think of intentional ways that you can put the other person first.
This is why one of the most effective ways to make new friends is to ask
questions. Be curious about others. For leaders, lead with curiosity. Think
of each question as a breadcrumb.

It may seem obvious, but different kinds of questions can be helpful in
different situations—so it's important to put yourself in the other person's
shoes. For example, if a friend had been ill, had surgery, or experienced
a loss we often want to do something as an act of kindness and support.

If you ask if you can help, they usually refuse because it is hard for many of us to accept help. But I've learned what to say and what not to say.

I don't say, "Can I bring over dinner?" I say, "When can I bring over dinner?" If you take the food over in containers or packaging that don't need to be returned, then that makes the gesture even more thoughtful.

One of the best ways to get to know a person is to meet one-on-one. I learned this technique from a faith-based social justice group called AMOS, A Mid-Iowa Organizing Strategy. Their process consists of one-hour meetings, real face time to help you go deeper than small talk.

Over time, you'll discover who they are, what matters to them, and what motivates them while listening for talents, interests, passions, and frustrations.

Even the concept of setting up a meeting just to get to know someone can be uncomfortable for some people. But it is an effective way to build relationships. Call it old-fashioned dating, but it works.

This process can be used in any organization—even families—where the goal is to develop stronger relationships beyond a superficial level. But it takes time, effort, and intentional thought to make it happen. It is an investment that pays dividends.

Lyle Lynn was great at one-on-ones. Lyle was a friend and long-time member of our church. At his funeral a few years ago, there were about 300 people. Four people delivered eulogies—each from a different generation. This is not typical because Lyle lived to 93.

At that age, it's probable to outlive most of one's friends and family. But Lyle was a pro at cultivating and sustaining intergenerational relationships. He was proud to mentor people of all ages, and although he knew his time was limited, he did not slow down. Even in the last month of his life, his calendar was fully booked with lunch dates.

When Lyle was in the hospital, my husband and I went to visit him. I was chairing the stewardship committee at our church, which Lyle had done several times. He started asking me several questions related to the stewardship campaign. I said, "Lyle, we are here to see you. That is not important." He proceeded to coach me by sharing his wisdom about fundraising. That was Lyle and we were just two of the many people who benefited from his mentorship.

Relationships are important, but it matters with whom you surround yourself. When you are trying to make new friends, pay attention to how kindly they treat the people around them, and pay attention to what qualities they bring out in you. Better yet, surround yourself with people you want to become.

It's also worth paying attention to how homogeneous your social circle is. Over the course of a lifetime, too many of us choose to surround ourselves with people very similar to ourselves. We could learn a lot more from those who look at the world differently.

Breadcrumb Box:

I interviewed Dorie Clark, author and executive coach, who is part of MG100. She shared with me how Marshall Goldsmith is leaving his legacy.

Goldsmith went to a workshop and they used the Ayse Birsel book *Design the Life You Love*. One of the exercises was to think of heroes in your life and explain why they were heroes. The purpose of the workshop was to reflect on how you could be more like them. He thought of Peter Drucker and Frances Hesselbein, how they were generous and so helpful to him.

Goldsmith decided to give away his knowledge. He would adopt 15 up-and-coming executive coaches. There was lots of interest—16,000 people went through a formal application process! In 2016, he invited 100 people to join this small community, MG100.

He only had a handful of rules to govern this group. No guilt and no obligation. No pressure. Participation was voluntary. Members had to be nice and helpful. Nothing was done for money. But on one condition: you needed to find a way to share your knowledge and pay it forward.

This is a perfect example of legacy work. Goldsmith's goal is to teach people everything he knows. He was intentional about creating a community focused on giving back. He told Clark, "One day, you will be old like me, and you need to find a way to pass it forward."

Relationships Are Not Easy—At Home or at Work

Breadcrumb by breadcrumb, we have a choice in what we say, how we say it, and how we behave. We have a choice in what others think of us and remember about us on a daily basis.

We are also able to choose the way we approach relationships, especially if we feel we have made a mistake. All relationships have the potential to be messy, brought on by emotions, expectations, and misunderstandings. Recall the 5:1 ratio: there's a good chance that we may need to learn how to repair relationships that are important to us.

Understanding how to forgive yourself and others is a powerful gift. Easy to say, but not easy to do. According to a report by Johns Hopkins Medicine, forgiveness is a choice we make, and one that can have a direct impact on our health—it can decrease the risk of heart issues; lessen stress, depression, and anxiety; and improve sleep.

But most importantly, forgiveness is a skill you can learn and practice to improve your relationships—both at work and at home.

As a hospice volunteer, I go into homes to sit with patients and give caregivers a break (like anyone, caregivers need care, too). One patient,

"Susan," was confined to her bed. While she was limited physically, she was mentally sharp. I visited her weekly for nine months.

During the first week, Susan shared with me that she was estranged from her son, James. She told me how he was a big bodybuilder, strong, stubborn, and angry. While she was close to her adult daughter, she had not seen James in years. I came to learn that it was her husband, "Bill," who had a falling out with the son. Susan said that Bill would not hear of making amends.

After meeting with Susan for several weeks, it became clear that reconciling with James would make her happy. When I spoke to Susan's daughter, I realized that James had no idea how seriously ill Susan was. With her daughter's permission, I encouraged Susan to dictate a letter to James, which I would transcribe for her. It didn't matter if we sent it, but it would be a space for her to tell James what she wanted him to know before it was too late.

Once we set this "wheel" in motion, other conversations followed. It was about eight months later when Susan told me James came to visit her and she was beyond happy. A few weeks later, she was admitted to a hospice home.

The last time I saw Susan was the night before she passed. This big man with shoulders about a yard wide came over to me crying. It was James. He thanked me for breaking the ice so that he could see his mom a few times before she died. I told him how much he meant to her, how much she talked about him, and how reconnecting with him was her main dying wish. I only started the ball rolling.

Breadcrumb Box:

Dave Richo, psychotherapist and authority on relationships, summarized how to create positive relationships at work and at home in what he called the 5 "A's" of original needs in life. Throughout life, we have the same needs:

- Attention. We want someone to pay attention to our wants and feelings.
- Acceptance. We want to be accepted for who we are.
- Affection. We want to be shown the appropriate affection given the relationship.
- Appreciation. We want to be valued for the good we do.
- Allow. We want to make our own choices.

Expanding Your Circle

Social isolation can be an issue for any age, but it is particularly important to confront it as we age—and we are all aging. Our social circle tends to naturally shrink as people retire and leave the workplace, decide to move to warmer climates or to be closer to their grandchildren, experience illness, and even death.

The key is to be intentional about expanding your circle of friends.

Daniel Pink in his book *The Power of Regret: How Looking Backward Moves Us Forward,* discovered four core regrets—foundation regrets, boldness regrets, moral regrets, and connection regrets. His book is based on the largest sampling of American attitudes about regret as well as his own World Regret Survey (which has collected regrets from more than 16,000 people in 105 countries). Pink calls the four regrets a "photographic negative" of the good life. "By understanding what people regret the most, we can understand what they value the most."

Interestingly, connection regrets were the largest category—relationships that are fractured, incomplete, or ended. It takes time, energy, and effort to cultivate and sustain relationships. But the outcome is worth the investment.

While not always easy because we are creatures of habit, here are some tips to get you thinking:

- Join groups with like-minded people—for pleasure such as bike riding or for causes such as climate change.
- Reach out and develop intergenerational friendships. This will help you find balance and learn from different perspectives.
- To get those friendships started, invite people to coffee for one-on-one conversations. This is the best way to get to know people of all ages.
- Create new groups that meet regularly—such as a book club or a monthly dinner—and invite people you don't know so well.

Regardless of age, it is critically important to surround yourself with positive and optimistic people. Dan Buettner, author of *The Blue Zones,* created a quiz to help people maximize their health and happiness. The higher a person scores, the higher their quality of life is—which he says is linked to the number of meaningful social connections in their immediate network.

"In general, you want friends with whom you can have a meaningful conversation," he said. He advises people to focus on three to five real-world friends rather than distant Facebook friends. "You can call them on a bad day, and they will care."

Building community by being good "neighbors" is essential to stave off social isolation.

After reading *The Lost Art of Connecting: The Gather, Ask, Do Method for Building Meaningful Relationships,* I reached out to its author, Susan McPherson. She told me that healthy relationships involve reciprocity. Too often people consider networking to be the same as connecting, but she believes they are different activities.

"We all have superpowers, connections, and resources to help others," McPherson told me,

> but when we ask how we might be of help, we need to listen and most of us are not good at listening. Take what you learn from listening and follow up. This is a humane way to build relationships of credibility and trust.

A recurring question that crosses each phase of her method is this: *How can I be of help?* In contrast, many people approach networking with this question: *What can you do for me?*

McPherson concluded, "Everything good that has ever happened to me was the result of relationships from years of staying connected."

Breadcrumb Box:

"Legacies can be about big picture issues, but often they start small," says Deborah James, author of *Aim High: Chart Your Course and Find Success*, the 23rd Secretary of the Air Force, and the second woman to lead the military service in the United States.

For James, legacy has been about mentoring others along the way. Since she was fortunate to have good advisers and sponsors, she wanted to pay it forward:

> Grow where you are planted. Be a great mentor when and where possible. It is important for leaders to be role models in leading a full life beyond work. This can mean talking about family and not sending emails at all hours of the night. Be a reflective practitioner and pay attention to the impact of what you are saying and doing.

Build Neighborhoods at Work

After decades of surveying companies, Gallup created the Q12 survey to poll more than 25 million global employees and assess their engagement as accurately as possible.

Researchers linked the two following statements to increased employee engagement:

* I have a best friend at work.
* My supervisor, or someone at work, seems to care about me as a person.

These two sentiments reflect why a sense of community matters. People are more engaged when others care about them. Gallup links increased engagement to improved financial performance through a direct connection to increased employee productivity, retention, and organizational profitability.

Leaders are architects—both in building relationships and in creating the physical space where people spend most of their waking hours. Leaders should pay attention to the environment in which they expect their employees to work.

Sometimes, it feels like Generation Xers and millennials have seen the movie *Office Space* way too many times. They don't want to be stuck in a cubicle. Consider the recent trend toward open office plans: they want spaces that facilitate building relationships and connecting.

Since the pandemic, there has been a paradigm shift in the way that we envision an office. Many employees are accustomed to working from home, or as part of a hybrid model. While the setup of offices has changed, what people want from work—a sense of belonging—has not changed.

Dave Ulrich, author of *The Why of Work,* finds the concept of "belonging" a critical factor for creating organizational cultures where people thrive, not just survive. When we feel strongly bonded to another person or organization, our well-being will improve, and along with it, our performance and productivity.

Ulrich believes there are four key requirements of belonging:

Work and effort. Leaders who are too busy tend to erode belonging. It takes time and effort to invest in building relationships that work.

Put the "social" in "social media." Utilize technology to share more personal experiences so people get to know one another at a deeper level. In other words, "build connections, not contacts."

Empathy. Leaders need to understand and feel what others are experiencing. This can be done by asking others how you might help them or being aware of their personal circumstances.

People are agents for themselves. Leaders can shape personal accountability by helping employees shift their perspective. Instead of asking, "Do I like my pay, boss, or working conditions?" they'll wonder, "Do I do my best to earn my pay, build a relationship with my boss, or improve working conditions?"

Earlier in the book, we learned from Erica Keswin about how rituals can strengthen workplace culture. Leaders need to create spaces where people want to work. As architects, we need to facilitate the process of employees getting to know one another.

Keswin said we should lean on rituals to keep us grounded in turbulent times, both at home and in the workplace. Rituals are ways to celebrate wins—big and small.

When I asked Keswin how she would connect rituals with legacy, she shared this story:

> When I was interviewing people for my book, I came up with a question that helped me help leaders know what I meant by ritual. The question was: "What makes you feel most like..." And then I would add the name of the company, such as Chipotle. What makes you feel most Chipotle-ish?
>
> Legacy is what makes you feel most like you. Rituals that leaders create and sustain will be part of legacy—part of the legends people will tell after they are gone or even while they are still there.
>
> When my kids think about their childhood, what will they remember? What made our family feel like us: memories and stories. Traditions feel more like obligations versus a ritual which is a choice. I am amazed at how hard people will work to maintain rituals that are meaningful to them and the ritual may be goofy to people outside of the family or organization.

Rebuilding a culture where one feels a sense of belonging is a challenge. Leaders are struggling with how to put their organizations back together after the pandemic. Many workplaces have shifted to hybrid or fully remote models; leaders need to be intentional about investing the time and energy needed to "weave" people together, even when apart.

Be a Good Neighbor

To celebrate the 50th anniversary of *Mister Rogers' Neighborhood*, the documentary *Won't You Be My Neighbor* was made. To date, it is the top-grossing biographical documentary of all time. Then Marielle Heller's movie *A Beautiful Day in the Neighborhood* was released. Based on a famous *Esquire* article about Rogers, it stars Tom Hanks as Mister Rogers, known offscreen as Fred Rogers.

Because of the growing widespread loneliness epidemic, I was obsessed with reading everything I could about Mister Rogers. He was a great example of how being a good person makes you a good leader, and I devoured the lessons learned from a life well-lived.

I asked a colleague of mine who is also a movie buff what he thought of *Won't You Be My Neighbor*. He replied, "It conveyed the power of what can happen when you truly engage another person's humanity, without making excuses for them."

All of this research led me to summarize some leadership lessons from Mister Rogers. Since my definition of a leader is a person in a position to influence the lives of others, these lessons apply if you are a boss, parent, coach, teacher, or pastor.

1. **Slow down and focus.** After watching hours of recordings, Hanks said he realized that "Mister Rogers was always talking to a single kid, a single person two feet on the other side of the camera screen. They said when you were talking to Fred, you felt as though you were the only person in the world who mattered to him."
2. **Choose words carefully.** Every word was important to Mister Rogers and he chose them carefully. For example, he always used the word "program" to describe *Mister Rogers' Neighborhood*, as opposed to "show." This was important to his vision for the program's atmosphere.
3. **Be comfortable with silence.** Not only was Rogers' pace slow, but he demonstrated how to be comfortable with silence. This is basically a mindfulness/meditation practice. He used silence as a way to listen to others instead of monopolizing the speaking himself.
4. **Create rituals.** From the moment Mister Rogers walked onto the program, his behaviors were consistent, so the audience knew what to expect. This helped him create rituals that the audience could anticipate and look forward to, which fostered a community around the program.
5. **Validate all feelings.** Fred empowered the audience by validating all feelings. Rather than deny them, it was more important to know how to handle feelings in a healthy manner.
6. **Be authentic.** There is a line in Heller's movie that is significant. The *Esquire* reporter asks Rogers how different he is from the "character" he plays in the show. Rogers replies that he's not a character—the person we saw onscreen was who he really was.
7. **Be curious by being interested.** Mister Rogers was curious, which comes across in his love of asking questions. He understood that the practice was a great way to learn and to teach. He was driven by curiosity about people, places, and numerous topics—even difficult ones, like war, divorce, and death. He was the perfect example of how *being interested is interesting.*
8. **Create.** "I think that the need to create has to do with a gap," Rogers once said. "A gap between what is and what might be. Or what you'd like to be. I think that the need to create is the need to bridge that gap." Mister Rogers was inexhaustible creatively: according to Jeanne Marie Laskas in the *New York Times Magazine*, he was deeply involved in the program's screenwriting and wrote the music's melodies and lyrics. Through his creativity, Mister Rogers was trying to make viewers comfortable enough to express themselves, too.
9. **Demonstrate compassion.** "He knew the importance of bringing yourself to a child's level," Lynn Johnson, who spent over a decade photographing Rogers, observed in an interview with *NPR* journalist

Cathy Newman. "To speak *with* children, never *to* them." People of all ages and backgrounds were equal in Rogers' eyes.

10. **Show gratitude.** "He'd ask everyone to close their eyes for a minute and think about those who have been helpers in their lives," Johnson recalled. Focus on the "other" rather than the self.

When she was 25, journalist Jeanne Marie Laskas was sent to interview Rogers, and they became lifelong friends. When Rogers died of cancer at 74 in 2003, Laskas wrote an article about their relationship for the *Washington Post*.

"I know anything worthwhile I do as a parent is rooted in Fred's teaching about tending soil," Laskas wrote. "The same goes for anything good I do as a teacher... I've been working to create an atmosphere that allows people to be comfortable enough to be who they are."

"But it's all connected," Laskas continued.

> The soil, the atmosphere, the fundamental human urge to create. It all goes back to Fred's notion of a gap between what is and what might be. For Fred, creating is an expression of optimism, an act of faith. Faith in progress, in invention, in some basic urge to constantly make life better.

Perhaps the best way to understand how radical this message can be is to envision what happens when soil isn't tended. A barren landscape. A toxic terrain. An atmosphere lacking in love and acceptance, leading to struggle.

The 50th anniversary focus on Misters Rogers was all about his legacy, and he was the perfect example of a servant leader. He helped people feel good about who they were, and lifted them up. He demonstrated an unwavering commitment to the value of kindness. He left breadcrumbs for decades that people continue to remember.

With Rogers' memory in mind, one question to ask yourself after every interaction is, *Did I leave that person feeling better than before?*

Wisdom can't be taught, but it can be shared. My professional mentor, Dr. Elmer Burack, was my Mister Rogers, my Morrie Schwartz (as in *Tuesdays with Morrie*). I would not have published any of my books or grown in the ways that I did if were it not for Elmer. Every time I saw him, I expressed my gratitude and I never wanted our conversations to end because of the wisdom he would always share.

The quality of your relationships determines the quality of your life.

Back to the story about the couch. When I told my husband he needed more friends, he did not get defensive, but asked for my advice. Since he loves to read, I suggested he start a book club. Invite a few friends and then have each one of them invite one new person. In other words, I encouraged him *not* to invite the people he already knows so well so that he would increase his circle of friends.

As Arthur Brooks says in his book *From Strength to Strength*, men tend to have *deal* friends instead of *real* friends.

Society allows women more freedom to gather in groups than men. For this reason, women tend to have more social connections through book clubs, wine groups, and others. But after about four years, my husband's book club is a success. There are now 12 members who don't want to miss a single meeting. New friendships have formed. Interestingly, some other men have expressed an interest in being included.

Creating this club was out of my husband's comfort zone, but he thanked me. Now he has several friends who could help him move the couch.

Breadcrumb Ingredients for Building Relationships

Community Activities:

Plan events that bring people together in a community setting. Good examples are bowling or square dancing—any activity that does not require talent. Everyone can participate and join in the fun. These events facilitate getting to know new sides of people.

Intergenerational Mentoring:

Give and take. What do you know that you could teach someone else? What do you want to learn, and who can teach you? Reach out—especially across generations—and make it happen.

One-on-One Meetings:

Identify someone you want to know better. If you know the person, you might want to get to know him or her on a deeper level. Invite this person out for coffee. Explain there is no agenda. Then start asking questions about topics that are non-threatening—interests, hobbies, activities.

Talent Show:

Host a talent show for people to demonstrate their talents on a volunteer basis. Encourage a wide variety of talents such as readings, singing, playing instruments, even juggling. Imagination and creativity soar along with relationships as people realize hidden talents and common interests.

No Talent Show:

Host a "No Talent" show for anyone to demonstrate anything they want. Some people might be intimidated by the word "talent." But you can learn as much and have as much fun from people who are willing to share something that interests them.

Ask Questions:

Relationships form when we know each other. A great way to get to know people and to start conversations is to ask questions. A good place to start is with someone's office space. People decorate their space with artifacts, photographs, and mementos that are important to them. Each item can cue up a question and conversation. Be interested in others—and asking questions is a good way to show interest.

Listen:

Stop talking and start listening. Paying attention is a way to show respect for others, a sense of curiosity, and even humility. Sometimes we don't have to have the answers or to offer advice. We just need to listen.

Tending the Soil:

How well are you "tending the soil" for the people under your influence? This involves examining your environment at home or at work. Are the conditions conducive for cultivating and sustaining healthy relationships?

Start a Book Club (or Any Club with a Focus of Interest):

Invite two to three people who enjoy reading and who you'd like to get to know better. Then ask each of them to invite two to three people of their own choosing. Develop a system of selecting the books and a schedule of who will host each meeting.

Bibliography

Brooks, A. C. (2022). *Strength by strength: Finding success, happiness, and deep purpose in the second half of life*. New York: Portfolio/Penguin.

Buettner, D. (2010). *Blue zones: Lessons for living longer from people who've lived the longest*. Washington, DC: National Geographic.

Cherches, T. (2020). *VisuaLeadership: Leveraging the power of visual thinking in leadership and life*. New York: Post Hill Press.

Coughlin, J. (August 24, 2021). "Got friends? 4 questions about retirement planning, true social security and social media." *Forbes*. https://www.forbes.com/sites/josephcoughlin/2021/08/24/got-friends-4-questions-about-retirement-planning-real-social-security--social-media/?sh=2753b7016f26

James, D. (2019). *Aim High: Chart your course and find success*. New York: Post Hill Press.

John Hopkins Medicine. (n.d.). "Forgiveness: Your health depends on it." https://www.hopkinsmedicine.org/health/wellness-and-prevention/forgiveness-your-health-depends-on-it

Judge, M. (Director). (1999). *Office Space*. [Film]. Twentieth Century Fox.

Keswin, E. (2021). *Rituals roadmap: The human way to transform everyday routines into workplace magic*. New York: McGraw-Hill.

Laskas, J. M. (November 19, 2019). "The Mister Rogers no one saw." *New York Times Magazine*. https://www.nytimes.com/2019/11/19/magazine/mr-rogers.html

McCain, J. (January 28, 2008). "John McCain, prisoner of war: First person account." *U.S. News & World Report*. https://www.usnews.com/news/articles/2008/01/28/john-mccain-prisoner-of-war-a-first-person-account

McPherson, S. & Ashton, J. (2021). *The lost Art of connecting: The gather, ask, do method for building meaningful relationships*. New York: McGraw-Hill.

Mineo, L. (April 11, 2017). "Good genes are nice, but joy is better." *The Harvard Gazette*. https://news.harvard.edu/gazette/story/2017/04/over-nearly-80-years-harvard-study-has-been-showing-how-to-live-a-healthy-and-happy-life/

Murthy, V. (2020). *Together: The healing power of human connection in a sometimes lonely world*. New York: HarperCollins.

Neville, M. (Director). (2018). *Won't You Be My Neighbor?* [Film]. Tremolo Productions,

Newman, C. (February 8, 2020). "The man behind Mister Rogers, away from the neighborhood of make-believe." *NPR*. https://www.npr.org/sections/pictureshow/2020/02/08/803320785/the-man-behind-mister-rogers-away-from-the-neighborhood-of-make-believe

Pink, D. H. (2022). *The power of regret: How looking backward moves us forward*. New York: Riverhead Books.

The power of Gallup's Q12 Employee Engagement Survey. (2021, September 11). *Gallup*. https://www.gallup.com/access/323333/q12-employee-engagement-survey.aspx

Putnam, R. (2001). *Bowling alone: The collapse and revival of American community*. New York: Simon & Schuster.

Stillman, J. (July 31, 2020). "Use the magic 5:1 ratio to improve all your relationships." *Inc.* https://www.inc.com/jessica-stillman/use-magic-51-ratio-to-improve-all-your-relationships.html

Ulrich, D. & Ulrich, W. (2010). *The why of work: How great leaders build abundance organizations that win*. New York: McGraw-Hill.

Chapter 7

Enjoy Every Sandwich

The rock singer-songwriter Warren Zevon appeared on *The Late Show with David Letterman* soon after he found out he was diagnosed with pleural mesothelioma, a diagnosis that meant he only had months to live.

"I'm working harder," he shared.

> I mean, you put more value on every minute. You do live. I mean, I always thought I did that, I always enjoyed myself, but it's more valuable now. You're reminded to enjoy every sandwich, and every minute playing with the guys, and being with the kids and everything.

Breadcrumb Legacy is about realizing life is only made up of moments. It is about enjoying every sandwich—and every bite.

As Zevon says, if we are going to enjoy every breadcrumb that makes up a lifetime of sandwiches, it is critical to incorporate resilience into our lives. We need tools and practices to overcome the negative effects of the ego. We need to know how to feed the "dog" more than the "wolf."

The power of resilience is clear in the 1953 short story "The Man Who Planted Trees" by the French writer Jean Giono. It describes how a shepherd named Elzéard Bouffier gave life back to a desolate forest in the foothills of the Alps simply by planting acorns...many acorns.

Although this land did not belong to him, Bouffier began planting acorns three years after losing his only son and his wife. After five years, what was once barren countryside is now filled with oak trees. The trees set off a chain reaction, leading water to flow abundantly and restore the countryside. Families moved back to the newly thriving area. They rediscovered their purpose for living because they were given hope.

Bouffier's story is a great example of the progress principle. When facing challenging times—existential threats, crises, health issues, trauma—we need to find hope. But we also have to learn to be hopeful. The international service organization Optimist National has seen membership decline ever since its peak in the 1990s, with 1,088 regional chapters folding in the past decade and 13 in late 2020 alone. Even optimists are struggling to stay optimistic!

DOI: 10.4324/9781003310211-7

Hope accumulates: it lets us invest in the future. One breadcrumb of hope leads to another, and our fixed attitudes shift. If we are going to become the best people we can be and live in ways we want to be remembered, it is important we remain hopeful, use our creativity, and stay curious.

Every Sandwich—and Every Bite—Can Be a Small Win

Celebrate the small wins.

Karl Weick, the renowned University of Michigan psychologist, coined the phrase "small wins" as a way of reframing the scale of social problems. Instead of letting larger problems overwhelm us, we can break them down into smaller, more approachable steps. Then, they'll be more manageable to overcome.

The concept of small wins can be life-changing because the momentum of celebrating progress can increase our motivation and instill greater optimism. Each everyday success increases confidence, and is a breadcrumb that adds up to something larger. Acorns become oak trees.

Weick attributes the success of Alcoholics Anonymous to the fact that people are not asked to abstain for the rest of their lives, but rather to stay sober for a day at a time or even an hour. The same logic can be applied to large social problems that can be so overwhelming that solutions seem impossible—unemployment, the healthcare crisis, or natural disasters. People often avoid addressing these issues or come up with comprehensive programs that fail.

When I share the concept of "small wins" in classes and workshops, I first ask people to name what would be a "big win" for them. People typically respond with life landmarks like marriage, graduation, having children, or their favorite sports team winning a Super Bowl or the World Series. Then I ask them, "How often do these big wins happen?" Usually they answer, "Not very often."

If we live for the big wins, we often live with disappointment, frustration, sadness. Celebrating small wins keeps us positive and hopeful.

To better illustrate the idea of "small wins," I like to reference the 1993 movie *Groundhog Day*. In the movie, Bill Murray's prickly character is condemned to repeat the same day over and over, and he goes through various stages of feeling trapped and depressed. Eventually, though, he is able to change his fate—and mature as a person—by changing his habits.

Life can be repetitive and mundane if we choose to view it that way. Instead of feeling stuck, we can develop practices that help us reenergize and renew ourselves. The key is to start small and to celebrate the small wins along the way.

Remember: Breadcrumb Legacy is about bite size pieces—breadcrumbs—and letting them accumulate. You'll build momentum in the direction you want by intentionally leaving behind a path that makes you proud.

Breadcrumb Box:

"I like the concept of Breadcrumb Legacy: One can't survive on breadcrumbs, but they accumulate into a loaf of bread, and that can sustain you," Todd Cherches reflected during our interview. He continued:

What you give of yourself is a breadcrumb similar to random acts of kindness. So many people go unrecognized, such as frontline workers. During COVID it was nice seeing people recognized as Essential Workers by the nightly clanging on pans and clapping in New York City. But during normal times, all workers should be considered essential.

What Prevents Gratefulness

Being mindful of small details means being aware of moments: that is, the importance of time.

When talking about time management in leadership courses and workshops, I often remind people that we don't manage time. We manage our energy and our behaviors in the context of time.

Interestingly, time is the one resource that is the most democratic. We all get the same 24 hours a day, but we don't know when our days will end. It may seem easy to say that life is about making the most of our breadcrumbs during our limited time—but we are *not* perfect people. We make mistakes. We get derailed. Our egos get in the way and want to take over.

Think of an oxygen mask: you need to put on your own before you can help someone else. In the same way, we need to take care of ourselves before we can take care of others—and in order to take care of others. We need to be able to breathe.

Gratefulness can help us do so. In her book *Wake Up Grateful: The Transformative Practice of Taking Nothing for Granted,* Kristi Nelson explains that gratefulness, rather than gratitude, is a perspective we can choose: it is a state of feeling gratitude for everyday life in general, rather than one specific event.

But Nelson also points out some major inhibitors to feeling grateful: unmet expectations, jealousy toward others, a scarcity mindset. Each of these can be addressed with awareness and intention: in other words, through practices, as we learned in Chapter 4.

Developing consistent practices takes time. Malcolm Gladwell reports in *Outliers* that it takes most people 10,000 hours to become excellent at a sport, instrument, or skill. Professional musicians and athletes are expected to hire coaches to give them honest feedback for improvement. Yet, most leaders often operate in a vacuum with little to no input from others.

But finding practices that will work for us is an essential step toward living our legacy. Like gratefulness, this process depends on recognizing our support systems. It's not solely about looking inward, but about evaluating feedback from the people you trust the most. When we do this, we can learn how to pay it forward and support others in the same way.

Breadcrumb Box:

Howard Behar, the former President of Starbucks Coffee Company International, shared an organizational legacy story that has become a legend. Jim was a customer who lived in a care center across from one of the Starbucks stores in California. Every day, someone would come into the store around 2:00 pm and order a short drip coffee and a blueberry muffin to take to Jim. This went on for about two years.

Since Jim was a former football player, the baristas would write something personal on the paper bag or the cup to lift Jim's spirits. Then, one day at 2:00 pm, no one came in. With every hour, the baristas wondered what happened. One of the baristas decided to take the coffee and muffin across the street to the receptionist to give to Jim.

When asked about Jim, tears started streaming down the receptionist's face: "Jim died last night in his sleep." Of course, all of the baristas were sad. But two days later, one of Jim's children came in and asked the store manager if all of the baristas could come to Jim's funeral. When they showed up at the funeral, there were three big round tables that would seat eight to ten people. On these tables was every cup and every bag that the baristas had inscribed for Jim! The little things in life help people feel important, not invisible.

I often think about this story as I walk down the street. I try to remember to not put my head down when I see someone, but rather to look up and say hello. Even when it might feel uncomfortably direct, I want to show that I care and acknowledge others.

How to Live a Life of Gratefulness

If we want to "enjoy every sandwich," we need to develop our awareness and engage in meaningful practices. The following sections outline some of the most valuable skills for living a life of gratefulness:

Creativity. Curiosity.

Years before Diversity, Equity, and Inclusion became a well-known acronym, I taught a college diversity course. The main objective was to learn how to work together comfortably and effectively to accomplish goals.

I defined diversity very broadly. We covered the typical "isms"—racism, ageism, and sexism—in addition to other forms of discrimination pertaining to religion, sexual orientation, disabilities, AIDS in the workplace, and even lookism. The syllabus was based on numerous articles, films, and guest speakers for each primary diversity dimension.

I would remind the students that we were not to judge or fear each other, but to ask questions. Be curious. You don't have to have the answers, but by asking questions, you demonstrate your interest.

Being inquisitive means that you are open to the world, which is essential to living a life of gratefulness. Recall what we learned about a growth mindset: a perspective that will prevent us from assuming we have the answers, instead energizing us to try new things, take lessons, and use each day to learn and grow.

As we discussed in Chapter 6, curiosity helps us start conversations and build relationships—we listen more than talk, which keeps us from making unfair assumptions about the other person.

As we grow older, it is easier to stay in our comfort zones rather than to venture out. It's easier to retreat inside ourselves with a fixed mindset, since asking questions means that we are vulnerable.

Why stop asking questions, even if we're still curious about them deep down? Did we assume that we should already know the answers—and the act of questioning shows weakness? And why do we respect a sense of wonder in little kids, but lose it as adults?

When I interviewed Rob Walker about his book *The Art of Noticing,* he said the goal should be to "get curious about getting curious." He noted that most organizations don't encourage employees to take risks, even though curiosity is essential for true innovation. How can anyone invent a creative solution without the curiosity to envision a different world?

Personally, I have found that genuine curiosity keeps one's mind open. So many things in life are not black and white, but gray. If we resist jumping to conclusions about people, places, and things, we can see with new eyes what we have stared at for a long time.

For this reason, I love organizational psychologist Adam Grant's practice of creating an "Ignorance List." Each day, he adds reminders of all that he still doesn't know, which keeps him in a mindset of discovery, growth, and learning.

You can discover and pursue the "mild and strange" curiosities in your own life by being mindful of your moments—the breadcrumbs you are leaving—and paying attention to the reactions and responses you receive from others. It's all about tuning your antenna to the world around you: instead of "seeing what happens," be alert to whatever signals you take in. A moment that initially seems insignificant may surprise you down the road, if you are open to it.

Courage. Forgiveness.

We typically associate courage with heroic and brave deeds. But the Latin root of the word courage is deeper than that: it is *cor*, meaning heart.

A CEO of a large bank stressed to me that leadership is a matter of having our hearts in the right place. "Isn't it true that what we know really well, we 'know' by heart?" he asked. "When we take something seriously, do we not 'take it to heart?' When one does something abhorrent, do we not say 'Where is your heart?' Yet, when we are discouraged, we 'lose heart.'"

"Conversely," he continued, "when we find courage, we have 'found our hearts.' When we send something in our entire being, we 'feel it in our heart.' And when we have learned something 'by heart,' we act on what we know."

Courage involves both heart and bravery. It takes courage to be a leader. It takes inner strength to be a good person and do the right thing. It takes a lot of heart to forgive or ask for forgiveness. And it definitely takes courage to be resilient when facing challenges and uncertainty.

To get in touch with what you are feeling—and what is in your heart—you need to tame your ego. As we discussed in Chapter 4, your ego is often not your amigo, and can behave recklessly to protect you.

One visual I often use is a snow globe. You can only see what is inside of the globe when the snow has settled. In the same way, your "monkey mind" can jump around and prevent you from being present.

Any self-reflective and contemplative practice can calm the monkey mind. This is often called doing the "inner work." In addition to yoga, there are many different activities that cultivate focus. The Drucker School of Management and Wharton Business School now offer instruction in mindfulness meditation, and companies such as Goldman Sachs, General Mills, Apple, and Google include it as part of employee development. Tai chi, drumming, prayer, and journaling are a few other ways you might alter your state of consciousness. As executive coach Dan Petersen once told me, "Creative breakthroughs often emerge during repetitive exercises."

By calming the ego, we also shake the defense mechanism of believing we are in the right, which makes us more inclined to forgive. Forgiveness takes courage, and as we learned in Chapter 6, it is the bedrock of mature, healthy relationships.

With practice, we can learn to forgive. It is a teachable skill that requires a high level of emotional intelligence (one of the Breadcrumb Ingredients at the end of this chapter will get you started). The ability to forgive also reorients our perspective toward growth and opportunity, rather than holding on to past resentments. This will help us embrace unseen potential for the future.

Delight. Grace.

Jesse Lyn Stoner, Founder of Seapoint Center, told me: "When you live in the way you want to be remembered, what comes back to you is gratitude and feelings of joy."

I first encountered the idea of a gratitude journal in *O*, Oprah's magazine. Starting in 1996, Oprah kept a daily gratitude journal for a decade by writing down five things for which she was grateful. Then life got too busy for her to keep up the habit. While she still wrote in her journal some nights, her ritual started slipping away.

Since 1996, Oprah had accumulated more wealth, more responsibility, more possessions; everything, it seemed, had grown exponentially—except her happiness. She had grown too busy to feel *anything*. But things began to shift when she began gratitude journaling again.

What changed? She made an *intentional choice* to feel gratitude. While building a television station, Oprah got so focused on the difficulty of the climb that she forgot her gratitude for simply having a mountain *to* climb. Only when she made a conscious effort to recognize this did a shift happen.

Research supports that practicing gratitude will have a positive impact on health, resilience, and performance. In one such study, Kim Cameron, the William Russell Kelly Professor of Management and Organizations at the Ross School of Business at the University of Michigan and thought leader on positive leadership, asked his students to keep a journal every day. Half of them would keep a gratitude journal, where they would log three things for which they were grateful or three positive highlights of their day. The other half of the students were asked to simply keep a daily event journal: a record of events and relationships, or problems they faced.

At the end of the semester, several studies were conducted. After giving everybody a flu shot, it turned out that students who kept a gratitude journal had more antibodies in their system than the others. The gratitude journal group also displayed greater mental acuity when asked to memorize information or create sophisticated rules to make difficult decisions. In fact, the gratitude journal students' grade point average was almost a half a grade higher than that of the other group.

Focusing on your blessings can help you maintain a more positive attitude, and Cameron suggests a simple way to start. First, think of all the bad things going on in your life. The problems you're facing. The stress you're encountering. Then, reframe your perspective by asking, "What am I learning? What should I be thankful for? How can I be thankful for even the most difficult situations?"

Personally, I have mixed feelings about gratitude. Oftentimes, gratitude can seem self-serving and even condescending. For example, it is easy to think or to say: "I am glad that did not happen to me…" "I am grateful I was able to…" "I am thankful I had the good fortune to…"

I had an awakening when I read *The Book of Delights* by Ross Gay. His practice was similar to gratitude journaling: he challenged himself to write "a daily essay about something delightful" each day for a year.

I was struck by the way Gay looked for joy that may not have had anything to do with him individually. Gay finds delight in the sight of grandparents spending time with their grandchildren. In watching someone enjoying an espresso while sitting outside at a cafe. In observing people on the subway being kind to one another. He is looking for moments to celebrate life in general—and paying attention to the breadcrumbs other people are leaving.

Recall that there is a significant body of evidence telling us that focusing on the good of one's organization—as opposed to oneself—enhances career success. So, instead of understanding gratitude as something linked to your *wants*, try shifting it to *others' needs*. Put differently, it's often more fulfilling to turn your attention outward and scatter breadcrumbs of kindness for others. Another way of paying it forward.

Laughter. Humor.

It helps to have a sense of humor. Even Viktor Frankl wrote in his endlessly enlightening book *Man's Search for Meaning* about the importance of humor in dark times. Frankl, who was a psychiatrist and Holocaust survivor, detailed his experiences in Nazi concentration camps and the role humor played in survival: it builds resilience and hope, and allows you to momentarily escape your circumstances.

Life was challenging for millions of people before, during, and after the COVID-19 pandemic. There is nothing funny about losing your job, living paycheck to paycheck, or living in a divided country or family because of politics. It's not funny when you find yourself mad or beating yourself up because you don't like who you are, or don't think you are who others want you to be.

Even if it can't resolve difficult circumstances, finding levity can help you face your challenges with newfound strength. In fact, humor is so important it is being taught at Stanford GSB by social psychologist Jennifer Aaker. She and her co-author Naomi Bagdonas wrote a book titled *Humor, Seriously,* and they shared some intriguing research in a 2021 interview published on Chip Conley's blog *Wisdom Well*.

They cited a 15-year longitudinal study of more than 50,000 Norwegians, which demonstrated that a good sense of humor can extend a person's life by eight years, about the equivalent of a heavy drinker giving up alcohol. If we embrace humor, those eight years will be both happy and meaningful. Laughing releases healthy hormones, like dopamine, that make us feel better; humor also makes us seem more likable and affable to others. Humor builds resilience, and with that, a sense of hope.

If humor is healthy, why aren't we smiling more? In the workplace, it is true we need to be professional, but we spend a large portion of our life at work so we might as well enjoy ourselves. There is very little downside to humor unless it is hurtful to a person or group of people. It is better to laugh *with* others. And self-effacing humor can be healthy to stave off self-seriousness.

Model Role Models

Finally, you can learn a lot from observing people who are living a life of meaning and purpose. Seek out those people who are living a life that looks healthy and appealing.

Several of my interview subjects—such as Robert Glazer, founder and CEO of Acceleration Partners, and Wayne Cascio, author of *Responsible Restructuring*—cited Herb Kelleher as a role model. Kelleher was the co-founder, former CEO, and chairman emeritus of Southwest Airlines until his death in 2019.

"Herb Kelleher was such a regular guy and successful in one of the most heavily unionized industries," said Glazer.

> He had strong relationships with employees. He would hold a barbe-cue for the mechanics who were working the night shift. He would meet with flight attendants in a diner after they got off work. He was so informal that he would seal agreements with a handshake or some-thing written on the back of a napkin.

Kelleher was trusted by employees and he always treated them with re-spect and dignity. Cascio remembered how a *Fortune Magazine* writer asked Kelleher what comes first: shareholders, customers, or employees. "Herb did not hesitate," he said.

> Employees always come first because if you treat them well, then they're going to treat customers well. And if you treat your customers well, two things happen. One is that the customer comes back and wants to do business with you. The other is the customer talks to his or her friends and encourages them to do business with you. Both ways are good for shareholders.

Likewise, Glazer defined legacy as "what comes after you." Glazer contin-ued, "what you create that sustains an impact after your lifetime." He said Herb Kelleher was a great example of someone who created a company culture that is pervasive and continues to live on.

So much can be learned simply by being aware and present. Kelleher reminds us that leadership is about being a good person: we demonstrate it when we live a life of gratefulness. It's all in the breadcrumbs we leave behind.

> **Breadcrumb Box:**
>
> When Kathy Robinson, the founder and director of career coaching platform TurningPoint, was working in the corporate world, she told me she did not think about legacy because she did not feel as if she had control over how her legacy would be remembered. She did, however, think about how she was being a good steward and if she was taking the company to the next level.
>
> "I wanted to advance the company while honoring and building on the past, so when the next person came in, they could take it to the next level," she explained. "I wanted to leave the company in a better place than when I came in."
>
> When I asked her to share a meaningful story about legacy, she immediately thought of her grandmother. "She was born in 1904 and Italian to the core," Robinson told me.
>
> > She grew up in Brooklyn, New York and never drove a car. In fact, she never lived outside of that one block. She lived to be in her 90s and was the epitome of love and resilience in a difficult life. She raised four kids in a three-room apartment.
>
> Robinson asked herself what it was about her grandmother's legacy that meant so much. "She was so content and joyful in all that she had, which was little from a material standpoint," she reflected. "I try to never lose sight of where I come from."

Small Steps Are Breadcrumbs

For many years, my academic research was focused on continuous quality improvement (CQI): the way people and processes depend on feedback to improve. My dissertation was on strategic planning in higher education, and I later co-authored two books and several articles on quality improvement in that field. I would tell my students that I had CQI in my bloodstream!

When I was researching continuous improvement, I had the opportunity to meet Harry Roberts, author of *Quality Is Personal: A Foundation for Total Quality Management,* at a professional conference. He was a distinguished professor at the University of Chicago and one of the leading authorities in total quality management.

But it was the title of his book that captured my attention, especially in relation to my findings on feedback. Organizations can only learn to function better as quickly as their people do. Quality really is personal. I took that concept to heart.

So how do we invest in our own improvement?

When I interviewed John Baldoni, author of *Grace: A Leader's Guide to a Better Us* and the more recent book *Grace Notes: Leading in an Upside-Down World,* he told me that his mantra is: "Focus on Better." "You get to define what 'better' means," he explained. "What can you do to be a better husband, a better spouse, a better friend, or a better colleague?"

Kaizen is a Japanese term meaning "change for the better," or continuous improvement. It is an ancient philosophy of using small steps to accomplish large goals. This is also the essence of *Breadcrumb Legacy*—paying attention to the small steps on our life journey. Through daily acts of compassion and curiosity, we can change ourselves and, eventually, those around us. But we can't get overwhelmed by the entire journey ahead: we have to build momentum by taking that first step, scattering that first crumb and celebrating each small win.

Think of a photomosaic: an image made up of many other tiny images. Up close you can see tiny, individual pictures, but when viewed from a distance, all of the images come together to create a completely different visual.

Imagine a photomosaic of your face made up of every person who works with you, your community connections, and others. The more clearly and consistently you approach your actions, the sharper your photomosaic will appear.

Your legacy won't be a report card of how you behaved or how your company performed. Rather, it will be embedded in the way that others around you think: a result of the time they spent interacting with you.

Your legacy is the difference you have made in people's lives, directly and indirectly, formally and informally. The challenge is how to create a legacy that others want to be a part of, too.

So try to see *Breadcrumb Legacy* as an ever-evolving process. The choices you make day after day, step after step—breadcrumb after breadcrumb— define the quality of your life.

Make sure you enjoy every sandwich.

Breadcrumb Ingredients for Enjoying Every Sandwich

Look for Humorous Moments:

Every day for seven days, write down the three most humorous things that happened that day. If you want more little moments of joy in your life, look for them. By doing so you'll actually be more inclined to see them, or even create them.

Seek Out Role Models:

Look for people who are living the legacy you want to live. What are their intrinsic characteristics? These are virtues such as compassion, gratitude, and honesty—*not* external motivators like money, possessions, and power. Through intentional effort, these virtues can be learned.

Now, think about small steps: what are some everyday ways that you can adopt these intrinsic qualities?

Notice Something New Every Day:

Many days we are like zombies, zoned out as we go through our routines. As you walk, ride, or drive, notice something new every day on your regular path. Houses, signs, street corners, even litter.

Meditative Breathing:

Inhale to a count of four. Hold your breath to a count of four. Exhale to a count of four. As you breathe, think of a mantra such as:

Inhale what you need,
Exhale what you don't need.
Inhale the present,
Exhale the past and future.

Write a Forgiveness Letter:

Write a letter that you may or may not ever send to someone who hurt you. Explain how you were affected by what was said and/or done. State what you wish the offender had done instead. Close the letter with a statement of forgiveness, understanding, and empathy—if possible. Another variation is to write the letter as if you were the offender who hurt someone.

Creativity Activity:

Make an intentional decision to learn something new that fits under the broad umbrella of "creativity." This can be something you used to do in the past that you would like to revisit, or it can be something totally new. The purpose is to "get out of your comfort zone" and do something that might enrich your life by reenergizing your spirit and energy level.

Bibliography

Aaker, J. & Bagdonas, N. (2021). *Humor, seriously: Why humor is a secret weapon in business and life.* New York: Currency.

Baldoni, J. (2019). *Grace: A leader's guide to a better us.* Pensacola, FL: Indigo River Press.

Baldoni, J. (2021). *Grace notes: Leading in an upside-down world.* Ann Arbor, MI: Baldoni Consulting, Inc.

Cascio, W. F. (2002). *Responsible restructuring: Creative and profitable alternatives to layoffs.* San Francisco, CA: Berrett-Koehler Publishers.

Chodran, P. (2002). *The places that scare you: A guide to fearlessness in difficult times.* Boulder, CO: Shambala.

Conley, C. (February 4, 2021). "Humor, seriously." https://wisdomwell.modernelderacademy.com/humor-seriously

Frankl, V. E. (2006). *Man's search for meaning.* Boston, MA: Beacon Press.

Garbarino, S. (February 5, 2021). "Optimist clubs see glass half full—Even in a pandemic." *The Wall Street Journal.* https://www.wsj.com/articles/optimist-clubs-see-glass-half-full-even-in-pandemic-11612539409

Gay, R. (2019). *The book of delights.* Chapel Hill, NC: Algonquin Books.

Giono, J. (2005). *The man who planted trees.* White River Junction, VT: Chelsea Green Pub.

Gladwell, M. (2011). *Outliers: The story of success.* New York: Little, Brown and Company.

Levin, M. (June 12, 2017). "Why Google, Nike, and Apple love mindfulness training, and how you can easily love it too." *Inc.* https://www.inc.com/marissa-levin/why-google-nike-and-apple-love-mindfulness-training-and-how-you-can-easily-love-.html#:~:text=Mindfulness%20meditation%20is%20a%20staple, Google%2C%20Apple%2C%20and%20Nike

Ludema, J. & Johnson, A. (June 12, 2020). "Now is the time to finally start practicing gratitude: Insights from organization culture expert Dr. Kim Cameron." *Forbes.* https://www.forbes.com/sites/amberjohnson-jimludema/2020/06/12/gratitude/?sh=77d7bf5267d3

Maurer, R. (2014). *One small step can change your life: The Kaizen way.* New York: Workman Publishing.

Nelson, K. (2020). *Wake up grateful: The transformative practice of taking nothing for granted.* North Adams, MA: Storey Publishing.

Pareles, J. (January 26, 2003). "Warren Zevon's last waltz." *The New York Times.*

Ramis, H. (Director). (1993). *Groundhog Day.* [Film]. Columbia Pictures.

Roberts, H. V. & Sergesketter, B. F. (1993). *Quality is personal: A foundation for total quality management.* New York: The Free Press.

Walker, R. (2019). *The art of noticing: 131 ways to spark creativity, find inspiration, and discover joy in the everyday.* New York: Alfred A. Knopf.

Weick, K. E. (1984). "Small wins: Redefining the scale of social problems." *American Psychologist*, 29(1), 40–49.

Winfrey, O. (November 2012). "What Oprah knows for sure about Gratitude." *Oprah.com.* https://www.oprah.com/spirit/oprahs-gratitude-journal-oprah-on-gratitude#ixzz6nQ2XYquh

Chapter 8

What Would Elmer Do?

As I began to write this last chapter, I came full circle. I started this book in memory of Elmer—my professional mentor and friend. He set me on this legacy journey. I was reminded of the gems of wisdom—breadcrumbs—that he shared with me, and which I now carry in me.

When I think of a life well-lived, Elmer is the first person who comes to mind. He was a great role model of living a Breadcrumb Legacy. He was so intentional about his most precious resource: time. In fact, I would say Elmer's purpose in life was to live with a growth mindset.

After Elmer retired from the University of Illinois-Chicago, he and his wife, Ruth, continued to take classes in all kinds of subjects, such as spirituality, philosophy, and history. Knowing Elmer, he probably volunteered to teach classes purely because he was interested in learning new things and sharing what he learned.

Elmer was curious. Since he and Ruth had been married for decades and were close, I assume Ruth was just as curious or enjoyed going along for the ride. He would describe to me how they enjoyed attending concerts at the Ravinia in Chicago; they'd take a picnic basket and folding chairs, and make an evening of experiencing live music with friends, regardless of who was performing.

Relationships were important to Elmer, but he was not a fan of email. Instead, Elmer would handwrite long letters with pages of research ideas, often suggesting additional articles for me to read. He would close with, "If you want to talk about these ideas, please give me a call."

He didn't do this to make it difficult to stay in touch. He believed that relationships were well worth the time and energy it takes to maintain them. Over our 20-year friendship, I kept all of Elmer's letters and often reread them as a way of keeping his wisdom and generosity close by.

Every time I went to Chicago, I tried to connect with Elmer. One summer, I told him I was going to a workshop in New York and that I had to

DOI: 10.4324/9781003310211-8

change planes in Chicago. He suggested, if I was not in a hurry, to arrange to have a four-hour layover so that we could have a long lunch.

Since Elmer lived in a northern suburb, I was honored he would go to this much effort to connect. He was running late to pick me up at the airport, and explained that he had to take Ruth home after their cancer support group meeting.

I was shocked. I had no idea he and Ruth were cancer survivors. Elmer responded calmly to my worried response. "Jann, don't worry. At my age, we call them bumps in the road. We deal with what we have to do and we keep going."

Even though Elmer was positive, optimistic, and hopeful, he embraced death. He also worked at keeping his ego in check. He was so accomplished and had many demands on his time. He did not owe me anything. It was a fluke how we met.

Since I was not one of his official graduate students, I always thanked him profusely. I would remember his birthday and send him little gifts in appreciation of his generosity and kindness. When the book *Tuesdays with Morrie* was published in 1997, I mailed a copy to Elmer because he was my Morrie. He would always say, "You have thanked me enough. Remember you are helping me to grow too. Friends help each other."

When Elmer died in 2012, I was not able to go to the funeral. But I called Ruth and asked if I could come visit her as soon as she felt comfortable. While I had never met Ruth in person, we often spoke on the phone and she would identify me as Elmer's "little friend from Iowa." From that visit on, when Ruth wanted to talk about Elmer, she would call me and we would reminisce about him.

Then Ruth died in 2017. I sent a long letter to the family with a memorial gift. One of her sons called me and we had a long talk about his parents. He closed by saying, "Both Dad and Mom thought of you as the daughter they never had. Please know they were so fond of you and they appreciated how you stayed in touch with both of them."

In an interview with Dan Rockwell for his blog "Leadership Freak," Luke Burgis, author of *Wanting: The Power of Mimetic Desire in Everyday Life*, explained the importance of a good role model. They teach us behavior—good and bad—and also reflect what is *worth wanting* in life. Wanting well, like thinking clearly, is not an ability we are born with, but it is something we learn.

Elmer was the whole loaf of bread! He was my main role model both professionally and personally, and by Rockwell's definition, he taught me what is worth wanting in life. I often ask myself: "What would Elmer do?" His legacy of wisdom lives on in me, for which I continue to be eternally grateful.

Breadcrumb Box:

A few years ago I was at a fundraising luncheon where a woman was honored posthumously. When her daughters accepted the award, one of them shared these comments. Her words are a worthy reminder of how we should pay attention to what we say and what we do; it matters in good ways and possibly bad.

I paraphrase:

"We may not know who is listening. We may not know who is watching. We may not know the influence we are having on others."

To which I might add: We need to live our lives as if others are listening and watching.

Be Wise. Share Wisdom.

Recently, I took an online course about wisdom through the Modern Elder Academy (MEA). When people shared something of value, we would rub our hands together as if we were shining their pearl of wisdom, the gem they just shared.

Like any good role model should do, legacy teaches us how to pass on the "pearls of wisdom" you have strung together throughout life. This book has taught you how every decision you make, every action you take, and every attitude you hold are breadcrumbs you are leaving behind. The hope is we are leaving breadcrumbs that are positive, because they will always have an impact on those we meet.

We are also living in a time when we are drowning in information and starving for wisdom. But what are some sources of wisdom?

In my Sage-ing work, we find that wisdom comes from processing our life experiences through some form of reflection. Wisdom can be gained from any activity that encourages you to contemplate the lessons you've learned in your life—for example, through journaling or meditation.

As I have said throughout this book, we often think of legacy at the end of our life, or when we leave a career: points of major transition. But wisdom can be passed on at any age, or any time in your life.

We've also talked about ways that your legacy can change the world for the better—in your immediate social circle, your workplace, even for acquaintances. Developmental psychologist Erik Erikson's concept of "generativity," is an adult's concern for and commitment to promoting the well-being of future generations. He argued that in the middle years of adult life we come to realize: "I am what survives me."

Wisdom entails realizing life is made up of moments—and that we have the power to choose how we act in those moments.

Breadcrumb Box:

In each of my interviews, I asked people to define legacy in a way that was meaningful to them.

Sinikka Waugh, president and founder of the training organization *Your Clear Next Step*, immediately responded that legacy is inherited, citing the work ethic that her parents and grandparents passed on to her.

"Legacy is what you remember from others," she told me. "Maybe you saw them model behaviors or they shared it with you. These are behaviors that I cherish and want to pass on. I want to 'channel' them and pass it forward."

As another cinematic example, I like to show my students a classic scene from *Dead Poets Society*. Set in 1959 at a fictional elite boarding school in Vermont, Robin Williams plays John Keating, a charismatic English teacher who inspires his students through his poetry lessons. (Teachers tend to enjoy movies about teachers.)

During a class discussion about the meaning of life, Keating quotes from Walt Whitman's poem, "O Me! O Life!" Then, he challenges the students to respond by asking them: "What will your verse be?"

Legacy is about asking, and answering, this question.

Grasping the concept isn't enough. You have to *practice* what you've learned—asking questions with openness, curiosity, and kindness—and incorporate it into your daily life. On average, it takes about two months to break old habits and create new ones. The time to start is now.

These three bullet points—which also tie together the most important themes in this book—will help you get started:

- **Gaining clarity** on how you'd like to live your legacy can give your life meaning and purpose.
- **Developing your legacy** enables your daily work toward your purpose, which influences how you show up in the world each day.
- **Thinking intentionally** about your legacy guides you to live your life in ways you want to be remembered.

Gaining Clarity on Your Legacy

Breadcrumb Legacy starts with purpose, but no one said it was easy to figure out what "purpose" means for you. It is easier to drift and blow with the wind. Without intentional thought, it is easier to live a life of indifference or indulgence.

One of the most important ways a purpose can help is by showing you how to allocate your precious resources of money, energy, and time—particularly time. The earlier you discover your purpose, the better off you are.

To find it, you have to work at it. Think—clearly, lucidly—about your hopes and dreams, what makes you happy, which relationships are positive forces in your life. Don't let life pass you by.

Recall that we can choose to live a life of significance. Your purpose gives discipline to your decisions, actions, and behaviors. Repeated behaviors become habits.

One visual metaphor for Breadcrumb Legacy is a wake of the boat: the trail we create in our lives. *Life on Purpose* author Victor Strecher says, "If your life is a boat, then you need a rudder to steer toward a harbor: an ultimate purpose."

Since we live our legacy each day, shaping our boats' "wake" also depends on how we show up in the world. Think back to our earlier discussions of mindfulness, where we emphasize "being awake" instead of sleepwalking through life.

So, discover your purpose by reviewing your gifts, passions, and values. Why are you going to get up in the morning?

Of course, your priorities can (and will!) evolve as you evolve, and change depending on your stage of life. Purpose is not necessarily a destination that is discovered once and for all. It can change as you do. It will not just fall into your lap!

Take this opportunity to experiment. Seek out and explore different organizations and hobbies. Find a cause that resonates with you and could use your efforts.

Gaining clarity on your legacy also requires you to think about *how* you want to be remembered. Simply put, if you want to live a life worth remembering, you need to be clear on what it will look like. This will help you stay deliberate in your daily actions.

Purpose is also about learning to become a nobody and *not* letting your ego get in the way. It's about investing in causes that are larger than you. Reflect on your talents and passions, then look outward to see where you might be able to apply them. Based on a study published in the journal *JAMA Network Open,* people who live purposefully—people who have a reason to get up in the morning—enjoy longer and healthier lives than those who don't.

Finding your purpose can sometimes seem impossible, as if you are seeking a faraway destination. But *every* moment can be purposeful, however small—and moments add up to days, days add up to weeks, weeks to months, and beyond. So, make it a purposeful day.

Developing Your Legacy

Margaret Newhouse, author of *Legacies of the Heart: Living a Life that Matters*, told me she defines legacy as "the footprint of our lives that lives on after our death and into another generation." But she made a point of expanding on this, telling me, "The *heart* is the key to a more positive legacy rather than ego-focused contributions, such as 'look at all that I have done with my life.'"

Throughout this book, I have described how your legacy is *ongoing*. We are leaving a trail behind us each and every day. In fact, our very presence is a breadcrumb: the way that we show up includes our attitude, perceptions, work habits, and more.

Relationships are essential as we embark on this journey. We may be called human *beings*—but we are really human *becomings*! As we've observed, the people with whom you surround yourself will shape who you are. If we want to become good people, we should not go it alone.

But why is it so hard to follow this old wisdom? We live in a disposable society. It seems easier to throw relationships away than it is to work on them. Some people feel relationships are not worth fixing. We want instant gratification.

In reality, relationships are messy and complicated, and they take time, effort, and persistence. With the passing of time, some people move, which means the relationship requires more work and effort to maintain; others die; and some relationships need to end because they are no longer healthy.

With relationships, it is not about quantity, but quality. We need to be intentional about cultivating supportive relationships, and be mindful of when they begin to turn toxic. And that work never ends.

Good relationships are not perfect, but they are crucial for our health and well-being. The quality of our life reflects the quality of our relationships.

When I interviewed David Bradford, co-author of *Connect: Building Exceptional Relationships with Family, Friends, and Colleagues,* he emphasized how "everything we do is a choice. The word 'can't' only applies to that which is physically impossible. Human interaction is a choice. We always have a choice of how we respond, and even not responding is a choice."

When developing your legacy, also work to get your ego out of the way. In workshops, I often use the metaphor of an elevator to explain ego. The ego will rise up to protect us, influencing us to say and do things that are not the best version of ourselves. When under stress, it is difficult to maintain control over our behavior. We can easily become defensive, jealous, micromanaging, or resentful, to name a few.

It is easier to control the ego and stay self-aware by changing your mindset from one of scarcity to abundance. When you view life through a scarcity lens, you compete for resources and you act out of fear. With an abundance mindset, you believe there are more than enough resources to go around. You are more likely to be compassionate and collaborative, not competitive and antagonistic.

Embracing death, rather than running from it, can help us reorient our mindsets away from limitations. Recall the wisdom of Sister Aletheia, the nun who wants us to stay mindful of death rather than avoiding it: an awareness of death will remind us of life's transience, driving us to make the most of today.

We may also need to "drop our tools" while developing our legacy. This has to do with a related shift in mindset toward growth, which emphasizes learning and improving. Instead of always trying to *prove* yourself, you can focus on *improving* yourself. This helps escape the trappings of a zero-sum world, and also helps you form closer bonds with others.

In other words, developing our legacy means we need to be awake to our thoughts and behaviors. If we have a tendency to seek approval or compete with others, then it is time to *drop* these mindsets and adopt a more positive perspective on life.

In the world of pop culture, we can find a voice of wisdom in the *Star Wars* film series. The legendary Jedi Master Yoda may be tiny in size, but his insight, kindness, and humor combine to make him an exemplar of *Breadcrumb Legacy*.

Some of Yoda's most famous quotes reinforce themes related to a growth mindset: they emphasize forging one's own path, choosing light over darkness, and going with the flow of the "force." What else is he? A positive role model and a mentor, devoted to passing his wisdom along.

To gain wisdom that is worth sharing, we need to let go of fixed-mindset behaviors that are defensive against the outside world. Don't focus on the destination, but on the process of evolving.

Thinking Intentionally About Your Legacy

We can't turn back the clock.

We will never have more time than we have right now.

In the book *Composing a Life*, Mary Catherine Bateson, an anthropologist and daughter of Margaret Mead and Gregory Bateson, examines the lives of five accomplished women with multifaceted careers, such as college president, psychiatrist, and electrical engineer. Bateson concludes their success was the result of the way they utilized their varied life experiences.

But what I found valuable about the book was the profound title: "composing a life." In the book, Bateson uses two metaphors: music and quilt-making. She describes how creating a life is like improvisational jazz, where musicians take bits of familiar melodies and rearrange them into a new piece. She also compares it to crafting a quilt or weaving, where threads are carefully trimmed to fit together and then sewn into a whole tapestry.

Breadcrumb Legacy is intended to help people of all ages and stages of life do just that: be deliberate about how we want to live our lives. With Bateson's metaphors as a guide, you can go about this by asking yourself two questions: What music do you want to create? What do you want your tapestry to look like?

In other words, *How do I want to be remembered? Am I living a life worth remembering? Am I living the way I want to be remembered?*

At a professional conference, I was struck by the clear passion for teaching and learning on display from one of the presenters, Susan Herman. She taught Organizational Behavior at the University of Alaska and was a natural leader. When possible, I always made a bee-line attending her workshops.

One year, I noticed Susan was not at the conference. I was told that she was battling pancreatic cancer, and I could follow her on CaringBridge, an online personal health journal. When Susan realized her time was limited, she immediately started sharing her favorite recipes on the platform with a brief story about each.

Even when she was hospitalized, she continued posting these breadcrumbs, up until she could no longer do it herself. Then Susan would dictate her recipes to her husband, who would share them, up until she passed away about six months later. Susan was intentional about leaving a meaningful legacy for those she held dear, recipe by recipe.

I interviewed Stew Friedman, author of the books *Total Leadership*, *Parents Who Lead*, and *Leading the Life You Want*, about these topics. He has been a professor of management practice at Wharton School of Business at the University of Pennsylvania since 1984 and is the founding director of Wharton's Work/Life Integration Project and Wharton's Leadership Program. Friedman explained how he has been teaching executives and students how to integrate life and work for decades:

> In my Total Leadership program, I ask participants to identify the most important people in the different parts of their lives, and describe what they think these people expect of them.
>
> They talk to these people to clarify their mutual understandings and to develop a keener awareness of how the various aspects of their lives affect each other. Then, they devise experiments intended to make things better in all the domains of their lives (home, work, community, and self)—to make the world better for others as well as for themselves.
>
> By taking this approach to leadership and change, people naturally focus on their legacy, on what they leave behind for those about whom they care most.

Each day, a Breadcrumb Legacy can take on a life of its own, steering and shaping your decisions, behaviors, and reactions. It reminds us to enjoy every sandwich: to celebrate our small wins, cheer on others, and, above all, to live a life of gratefulness. Like Elzéard Bouffier, we will plant trees under which we might not sit, but others will.

When we live a life of gratefulness, it is easier to find delight in the simple things. We gain momentum, hope, and inspiration to keep on the path. Recall the importance of finding humor and levity.

A buoyant spirit will also help you maintain curiosity and creativity, which depend on an open mind. Being curious can prevent you from being judgmental; it will allow you to keep a "beginner's mind" and a childlike sense of wonder. Being creative can prevent you from being bored. When you are more humble and get your ego out of the way—it goes without saying, don't be a know-it-all!—you are more receptive to new information and definitely more fun to be around.

The goal shouldn't be to cling to youth as you get older, but to keep your joy alive by nurturing your inner child. This will allow you to find purpose and engage meaningfully with a changing world.

Finding Strength in Vulnerability

Finally, it bears repeating: We are not perfect beings. We make mistakes. If you want to be a good person, you may need to apologize, forgive yourself, and forgive others.

People—and true leaders—demonstrate strength through a willingness to be vulnerable. We often hold grudges rather than address the issue, and it is sometimes easier to offend others and move on without mending the damage. As said previously, relationships can be messy, but they are worth the investment—in fact, we depend on that effort to thrive.

There is a story I often tell about my previous book *Leading with Wisdom*. When I submitted the final manuscript to the editor, one chapter was titled "Vulnerability Is a Strength." When he read that, he said that if I wanted to connect with men, I needed to change the title. "Men don't like to think of themselves as vulnerable because it feels like a weakness," he said. Based on his feedback, I changed the title to "Leaders Admit Mistakes Fearlessly."

Interestingly, Brené Brown's 2012 book *The Power of Vulnerability* helped to normalize the word. Since that time, all of her books have resonated with men as well as women. Acknowledging the power of vulnerability by name is here to stay.

Most people can "let go" and move on if there has been an acknowledgment of some injustice—intended or not. At times, we all must admit to not knowing the answers. Owning up to mistakes and seeking others' input requires humility. In fact, I think one of the greatest strengths a person can have is a capacity to acknowledge that they're in the wrong, and to ask for forgiveness if someone has been hurt.

Breadcrumb Box:

One of my fellow TEDxDesMoines speakers, Sara Maniscalco Robinson, gave a powerful talk. She is a veteran and she chose to speak about her experiences working with the Iowa Veteran's Perspective Charitable Foundation, a nonprofit organization that shares the first-person stories of Iowa's military heroes through film. As a global broadcast and print journalist for the military, she believes these stories need to be preserved for years to come.

I found Sara's talk particularly moving because she spoke about legacy without using the word. She began with a statement that I had not heard before, but which strongly resonated with me: "It has been said that people die twice. Once when their soul leaves their body, and the second when their name is said for the last time."

Since 1999, Sara has been wearing a POW bracelet with the name of an Iowan inscribed on it. Even though he was never found, he stays alive with her because she continues to say his name and share his story.

Our legacy consists of the stories people tell about us while we are alive and after we die. How can we live a life for which others want to tell our stories? A life worth continuing to say our name?

Breadcrumb Legacy as Your Yellow Brick Road

This book has taken me on a journey that I could not have imagined. Each decision to interview an expert, or the author of an intriguing book or article, led organically to the next interview. This is how I ended up interviewing Jesse Stewart, author of *Secrets of the Yellow Brick Road: A Map for the Modern Spiritual Journey*.

The Wizard of Oz has been one of my all-time favorite movies since I was a little girl. I loved everything about it: its music, sense of adventure, and characters. I wanted to have some ruby slippers. But it was not until I read Stewart's book that I truly understood the meaning behind all of the archetypes and symbolism in the movie.

Stewart explained how the whole film is about balancing the outer world with the inner world, which is why it has stayed so alive in our culture and our hearts. The movie takes us on Dorothy's journey—a spiritual journey—from her home in Kansas to the inner world of Oz. The catalyst was a twister that took her inward; the transition from her outer world to her inner world is represented by the film's shift from black-and-white to color.

Along the way, Dorothy meets three creatures who become her friends, but they each are seeking missing aspects of themselves: Scarecrow (a brain), Tin Man (a heart), and Lion (courage). They encounter good (the

Good Witch) and evil (the Wicked Witch). Life and death. When Dorothy wakes up from her dream, she realizes the farm hands in Dorothy's mind were made into the Scarecrow, the Tin Man, and the Cowardly Lion. The professor looks in through the window and Dorothy discovers he was the wizard.

According to Stewart, we need to face the challenge of the ego and engage with negative forces in the world. *The Wizard of Oz* teaches us how to move along the yellow brick road, toward our inner dreams, the possibilities that will make us whole. At the same time, there's no place like home. When Dorothy gets to Oz, she discovers that she had the power to go home anytime she wanted. She just had to go within herself.

I also asked Stewart how he thought *The Wizard of Oz* could guide the post-pandemic world. "The key to living is giving," he answered. "The more you give, the more you live. Be conscious of who you're spending time with and when, where, and the friends who you let into your world. Be more intentional. Stay awake."

You can learn a lot from practicing compassion and forgiveness. You can also learn a lot from observing the actions and words of others: Elmer was this role model for me.

You may not realize when your actions, words, and choices have an impact on others. Sometimes, we will never know.

Mildred Hastbacka, founder and managing member of Prakteka, told me she loved the image of breadcrumbs. "So many good things happen serendipitously," she said. "Our intentional scattering of breadcrumbs may be gold dust to us and they accumulate.

"Most of the monumental changes in my life came from reflections from others who may have thought them mundane at the time, but were powerful crumbs to me," she continued. "We had autograph books in 4th grade. There happened to be a substitute teacher at the end of the school year and I wanted to get her autograph. She wrote, 'Be good and you'll be happy.'"

Hastbacka told me, "Those few words had a major impact on me, and she likely did not even think about what she wrote. She might have written it in everyone's book. But I have remembered it for decades."

She reminded me how the words we speak are thoughts and ideas sent into the world. "If we never send our thoughts out," she explained, "they won't have a chance to take life into someone else."

Parting Thoughts

After teaching college for decades, I started compiling a list of my "thoughts" I wanted to share—particularly with graduating seniors. Eventually, I formatted and printed these thoughts on a card I distributed at the end of my course, consisting of all seniors.

After 30 years, I had a long list of thoughts:

1. **Embrace change.** Since change is inevitable, be flexible. Demonstrate creativity and your ability to adapt. This may involve accepting ambiguity and uncertainty.
2. **Focus on the questions and not the answers.** Uncertainty requires you to focus on the questions that need to be asked rather than looking for specific answers.
3. **Add value.** Always ask yourself if you are an asset to the firm or if you are a cost.
4. **Attitude influences everything.** Empower yourself by controlling your emotions and by being a positive force in your department or area.
5. **Always seek to learn.** Lifelong learning is the only way you can stay competitive in the market, whatever or wherever that marketplace exists. Develop a set of marketable skills that can be packed in your "suitcase" that you can take with you wherever you go.
6. **Quality is personal.** Take the quality principles and apply them personally just as organizations apply them. How can you continue to improve so that you add even more value?
7. **Self-knowledge is empowering.** The more self-aware you are, the more you can make the necessary adjustments to succeed in various situations.
8. **Create an environment where people want to work.** Great leaders make others feel great about themselves because the leaders have helped them to learn and to grow.
9. **Question assumptions.** Since diversity will only become more important, strive to be inclusive and fair. Often the right thing is not the easy thing in the short run.
10. **Celebrate the small wins.** If you live for the "big wins," you will continually be disappointed. Celebrating your small successes or those of others builds hope, patience, and momentum.
11. **Strive for excellence, not happiness.** If you are working toward excellence, you will be happy and find joy.
12. **Be an interested person.** An interested person continues to learn and is not bored. Developing many interests helps a person lead a more balanced life.
13. **Stay in touch with the people who are important to you.** They like you for who you are and not for who you know, how much money you make, or for the position you hold. It is easier to lose touch than it is to stay in touch.
14. **Listen to understand.** Active listening is hard work, but critically important. People need to know they are heard.
15. **Life is a series of choices.** Exercise those choices carefully. Try to anticipate the consequences. Take responsibility for the consequences of your choices.

Through this ritual of wisdom-sharing, I was imparting my legacy to the graduating seniors as they moved onto their next phase of life—through breadcrumbs, many accumulated breadcrumbs.

When I left my career as a professor, I created a bead necklace. I sent an email to friends, across the country and from various areas of my life, asking them to donate a bead or button (anything that could be strung) as a gift for the end of my career. The "beads" represent the support, wisdom, and courage from friends I treasure along my life journey. The necklace made as a result of these accumulated bits of friendship—"breadcrumbs"—was helpful to me in letting go and moving on to what was next. You can make something similar if intentional, forward thinking, and creative.

Breadcrumb Ingredients for Being Like Elmer

Good Luck It List:

Most of us are familiar with a "Bucket List": a list of things you want to do before you die. But now is the time to create a "Good Luck It List." This is a list of the legacy actions you want to leave behind that will give good luck to the world. Every day you can be leaving crumbs to make this happen. Make a list of the actions, behaviors, and initiatives you are taking now that will outlast you—and "survive you." *Thanks to Chip Conley.*

Make a Holistic Bucket List:

Draw five columns and label with these headings: learning, play, community, relationships, and spirituality. (Or, you can add your own categories.) In each area, list what you'd like to accomplish. This exercise helps you view life holistically.

Create a Bead Necklace:

Beads date back as far as 40,000 years. They are the earliest known artifacts that don't relate to daily necessities of life. Some historians think that the earliest beadwork was for religious purposes, but they were also used for protection, trade, money, and adornment.

Beads are similar to wise friends and Sages. They are burnished, polished, or highlighted by age, and come in numerous forms.

So, imagine (or create in real life!) a bead necklace that represents the support, wisdom, and courage from all of the friends you treasure along your life journey. Each bead reflects gems of wisdom and friendships. What is the story behind each bead? How do they differ in size, appearance, and texture? What qualities and characteristics are represented in each bead? This necklace or string of beads is a reminder of how breadcrumbs accumulate into something beautiful if we are intentional and awake.

Create Lasting Memories or Write a Memoir:

It is easy to self-publish photography books or memoirs. These books allow you to preserve memories through images or stories; they also encourage you to think deliberately about the wisdom you'd like to pass on. The key is to undertake these activities before the opportunity passes. Companies such as Storied Gifts specialize in capturing family history and life events.

Make a Bumper Sticker:

Design a bumper sticker that is six words or less that you would be willing to put on your car. It should reflect what you would want people to remember about you.

Invisible Tattoos:

Imagine tattoos were invisible. Share the words of wisdom you would have written on your body to guide your daily breadcrumbs.

To-Be List:

Yes, one more list. Instead of a to-do list, make a list of who you want to be—to become. To start, try brainstorming completed versions of this sentence:

I want to be _____.

Bibliography

Alimujiang, M., Wiensch, A., Boss, J., Fleischer, N. L., Mondul, A. M., McLean, K., Mukherjee, B., & Pearce, C. L. (2019). "Association between life purpose and mortality among US adults older than 50." https://jamanetwork.com/journals/jamanetworkopen/fullarticle/2734064 doi:10.1001/jamanetworkopen.2019.4270

Bateson, M. C. (2001). *Composing a life*. New York: Grove Press.

Bradford, D. & Robin, C. (2021). *Connect: Building exceptional relationships with family, friends, and colleagues*. New York: Currency.

Brown, B. (2012). *The power of vulnerability: Teachings of authenticity, connections, and courage*. Boulder, CO: Sounds True.

Burgis, L. (2021). *Wanting: The power of mimetic desire in everyday life*. New York: St. Martin's Press.

Freed, J. E. (2013). *Leading with wisdom: Sage advice from 100 experts*. Alexandria: ATD.

Friedman, S. D. (2014a). *Total leadership: Be a better leader, have a richer life*. Boston, MA: Harvard Business School Press.

Friedman, S. D. (2014b). *Leading the life you want: Skills for integrating work and life*. Boston, MA: Harvard Business Review Press.

Graham, R. (May 14, 2021). "Meet the nun who wants you to remember you will die." *The New York Times*. https://www.nytimes.com/2021/05/14/us/memento-mori-nun.html

Kershner, M. (Director). (1980). *Star Wars: Episode V—The Empire Strikes Back*. [Film]. Lucasfilm. Production.

Newhouse, M. (2015). *Legacies of the heart: Living a life that matters*. Narragansett Pier, WA: eBook Bakery.

Robinson, S. (May 11, 2021). *Life Lessons I Learned from Interviewing Veterans*. [Video]. *YouTube*. https://youtu.be/83wxl9Bv59Y

Rubin, G. (2012). *The happiness project*. New York: HarperCollins Publishers.

Slater, C. (January 1, 2003). Generativity versus stagnation: An elaboration of Erikson's adult stage of human development. *Journal of Adult Development*, 10(1), 53–65.

Stretcher, V. J. (2016). *Life on purpose: How living for what matters most changes everything*. New York: HarperOne.

Stewart, J. (1997). *The secrets of the yellow brick road: A map for the modern spiritual journey*. London: Sunshine Press Publications.

Weir, P. (Director). (1989). *Dead Poets Society*. [Film]. Touchstone Pictures.

Epilogue

After 30 years as a full-time tenured professor and then endowed chair in leadership and character development, I made the decision to "retire." But I prefer to use the phrase "move on" and continue to evolve. I wanted to write, facilitate workshops, and coach full-time rather than commute two hours a day and constantly grade papers.

About a month before I announced I was leaving to the faculty community, I had a professional academic conference in Chicago. As president of this academic organization, my expenses were paid.

Instead of flying, which takes about an hour in the air, I chose to ride the Megabus, which takes almost six hours. I planned to use the 12 hours of travel time to work on a project that was meaningful to me. This was my parting ritual, a way of infusing this life transition with deeper meaning.

I took a variety of about 100 of my homemade postcards and the faculty and staff directory. As I reviewed the directory, I proceeded to write notes to anyone and everyone who I wanted to thank. You could call them my "just because" notes, but they were part of my Breadcrumb Legacy.

In the notes, I did not mention I was going to be leaving the college. At that time, the college community had been my "family" for more than half of my life. My purpose was to make sure I thanked the people along the way who had helped me become the best teacher I could be—before they knew I was leaving. This included faculty members and staffers in technology, food service, maintenance, transportation, and more. I strove to add a specific example of their impact on me in each note.

After returning home, I dropped them into our interoffice mailboxes. For the next four weeks, many people would thank me as I would run into them. Only one person asked me, "Are you alright? You aren't ill, are you?"

After I announced I was leaving the college, people connected the dots. It was my way of creating a trail that mattered to me, and my way of letting go in order to move on. This career change was a death—many aspects of my life as I knew it were ending. You could say I had been in mourning the entire academic year.

DOI: 10.4324/9781003310211-9

It was a time-consuming project, but one that was worth the time and effort to show people that even their smallest actions helped me along my own journey. It is part of my legacy, of which I am proud.

This book is another such project: it is my legacy. I wrote it as if it might be my last book. Therefore, I wanted to make sure I included my best material. Since I could write a book on almost every chapter, it was hard to know where to end. But I know that readers now prefer shorter books.

I also envision this as a book with a shelf life, since these topics will always be timely and relevant. As long as people continue to question life, the major principles of *Breadcrumb Legacy* will live on within them. As we devote our time and energy to this great search, I suggest we approach life as seekers with a philosophy of "Living and Giving."

With the evolution of the Internet and social media, everyone has a big "megaphone" to broadcast their voices to the masses. Likewise, personal branding has become essential, and it's possible to make a career as an "influencer"—and a lucrative one at that.

But I would consistently warn my sons and my students about the downsides of the Internet, especially social media. It is very hard, if not impossible, to get something off of the Internet. Even when you purchase an item online, you are leaving a trail of your behaviors and habits, whether you realize it or not—a different kind of legacy.

Regardless of what I post online, I post it with the attitude that I want it to be there forever. It is part of my legacy. My sons are in a busy stage of their lives, but after I am gone they will be able to read what I was learning, thinking, and sharing.

I came to consider *Breadcrumb Legacy* as an analog trail. This simply means it's not digital, but it reflects your behaviors and habits just the same. They are imprinted on the minds of your family, friends, customers, and even strangers. This includes intended and unintended consequences.

My hope is to live a life and legacy that is inspiring and perhaps worth emulating in some ways.

Similar to all of our other breadcrumb interactions, joy accumulates—and if you're deliberate about spreading them, your crumbs will accumulate into a joyful loaf. Every day, I try to make sure the crumbs I am scattering about are good ones.

As a parting example, here is one final Breadcrumb Box:

Breadcrumb Box:

This is a postscript to my Breadcrumb Bags, some of the breadcrumbs I scatter around on street corners.

My husband, John, was following me home from an event—about ten minutes behind me. He came to an intersection and a homeless man was standing on the median strip with a sign in one hand and a granola bar in the other. John pulled up close to the side of the median strip and he could see a Ziploc bag of items that looked awfully familiar.

While waiting for the red light to change, John started talking to the man. He asked if he liked the bags of stuff, and he replied, "Yes, I like them. The granola bar I am eating came from the bag."

Then John said, "My wife passes out those bags and that looks like one of hers."

"A blonde woman just gave it to me," the man responded, "and told me that if I didn't want it, I was to pass it forward."

When he said that, John knew immediately it was me because I always say to "pass it forward if you don't want it." The man said, "Tell her thanks again."

Breadcrumb Legacy Manifesto

Having a PURPOSE gives meaning and direction to your life. It helps you decide where to leave your precious breadcrumbs of time, energy, and money.

Having a GROWTH MINDSET keeps you going and growing. As you evolve, so does your legacy—what you are leaving behind, and the difference you are making with your life.

Cultivating, nurturing, and sustaining RELATIONSHIPS is the key to happiness, joy, and meaningfulness. The investment of your breadcrumbs pays dividends.

Living a life well-lived involves EMBRACING DEATH. Breadcrumb Legacy means thinking about how you want to be remembered and living that life to the fullest right now.

Being your best self requires BECOMING A NOBODY. Your ego is not your amigo. You need to make sure the crumbs you are leaving behind are having a positive impact on others.

Living a Breadcrumb Legacy is about SHARING WISDOM that outlives you. This can be done by being aware and intentional of the breadcrumbs you are leaving for others to follow.

List of Interviewees

Jim Autry: Former president of the Magazine Group of Meredith Corporation. Author of *Love and Profit: The Art of Caring Leadership and Choosing Gratitude: Learning to Love the Life You Have*.

John Baldoni: *Grace: A Leader's Guide to a Better Us* and the more recent book *Grace Notes: Leading in an Upside-Down World*.

Suzanne Bates: Founder and Managing Director of BTS Boston and author of *All the Leader You Can Be*.

Howard Behar: Former president of Starbucks Coffee Company International and the author of *It's Not About The Coffee: Leadership Principles from a Life at Starbucks*.

Barbara Beizer: Co-founder of the Resilience Lab and leadership, transition, and life coach.

Ayse Birsel: Co-founder of Birsel + Seck, the award-winning design and innovation studio. *Author of Design the Life You Love: A Step-by-Step Guide to Building a Meaningful Future*.

David L. Bradford: Eugene O'Kelly II Senior Lecturer Emeritus in Leadership at Stanford University and co-author of *Connect: Building Exceptional Relationships with Family, Friends, and Colleagues*.

Kim Cameron: William Russell Kelly Professor of Management and Organizations at the Ross School of Business at the University of Michigan and authority on positive leadership.

Ron Carucci: Co-founder and Managing Partner at Navalent. Author of *To Be Honest: Lead with the Power of Truth, Justice, and Purpose*.

Wayne Cascio: Robert H. Reynolds Chair in Global Leadership at University of Colorado Denver Business School and author of *Responsible Restructuring: Creative and Profitable Alternatives to Layoffs*.

Peter Chatel: Founder of The Chatel Consulting Group and Georgia-based coachsultant.

Todd Cherches: Executive coach and CEO/Co-Founder of BigBlueGumball and author of *VisuaLeadership: Leveraging the Power of Visual Thinking in Leadership and Life*.

Dorie Clark: Executive coach and author of *The Long Game: How to Be a Long-Term Thinker in a Short-Term World*.

Sara Davidson: Journalist and author of *Loose Change: Three Women of the Sixties*.

Rachael Freed: Founder of Life-Legacies and a Senior Fellow at the University of Minnesota's Center for Spirituality and Healing.

Stewart Friedman: Professor at the Wharton School of Business at the University of Pennsylvania and the founding director of the Wharton Leadership Program and Wharton's Work/Life Integration Project.

Bill George: Former CEO of Medtronics, author of *True North: Discover Your Authentic Leadership.*

Robert Glazer: Founder and CEO of Acceleration Partners and author of *Elevate: Push Beyond Your Limits and Unlock Success in Yourself and Others.*

Marshall Goldsmith: Executive coach and author of *What Got You Here Won't Get You There.*

Ellen Goodman: Pulitzer Prize–winning journalist and co-founder of The Conversation Project.

Mildred Hastbacka: Author of *Channeling Wisdom: A Practitioner's Guide to Effective Mentoring in the Workplace.*

Tim Hebert: CEO of Trilix and author of *The Intentional Leader: How Inner Authority Can Unleash Strong Leadership.*

Sally Helgesen: Leadership consultant and co-author of *How Women Rise: Break the 12 Habits of Holding You Back from Your Next Raise, Promotion, or Job* and author of *The Web of Inclusion: Architect for Building Great Organizations.*

Deborah James: Former United States Secretary of the Air Force and the second woman to lead the country's military service and author of *Aim High: Chart Your Course and Find Success.*

Erica Keswin: Executive Coach and author of *Rituals Roadmap: The Human Way to Transform Everyday Routines into Workplace Magic.*

Jim Kouzes: Co-author of *The Leadership Challenge,* and Fellow, Doerr Institute for New Leaders, Rice University.

Janette Larkin: Former President and Publisher of Business Publications Corporation, Inc.

Mark Levy: Founder and CEO of Levy Innovation and author of *Accidental Genius: Using Writing to Generate Your. Best Ideas, Insight, and Content.*

Jack Maguire: Chair and Founder of Maguire Associates.

Susan McPherson: CEO of McPherson Strategies and author of *The Lost Art of Connecting: The Gather, Ask, Do Method for Building Meaningful Business Relationships.*

Harry "Rick" Moody: Former Vice President for Academic Affairs, AARP, and author of *The Five Stages of the Soul: Charting the Spiritual Passages That Shape Our Lives.*

Judi Neal: Judi Neal, founder and CEO of Edgewalkers International and author of *Edgewalkers: People and Organizations that Take Risks, Build Bridges and Break New Ground.*

Margaret Newhouse: Author of *Legacies of the Heart: Living a Life that Matters.*

Carol Orsborn: Author of *The Making of an Old Soul: Aging as the Fulfillment of Life's Promise.*

Parker J. Palmer: Founder and Senior Partner Emeritus of the Center for Courage and Renewal and author of *Let Your Life Speak.*

David Richo: Psychotherapist and author of *Shadow Dance* and *The Power of Grace: Recognizing Unexpected Gifts on Our Path.*

Kathy Robinson: Founder and director of the career coaching platform TurningPoint.

Rob Salafia: Author of *Leading from Your Best Self: Develop Executive Poise, Presence, and Influence to Maximize Your Potential.*

Tami Simon: Founder of Sounds True, a multi-media publisher dedicated to disseminating spiritual wisdom.

Jesse Stewart: Author of *Secrets of the Yellow Brick Road: A Map for the Modern Spiritual Journey.*

Jesse Lyn Stoner: Founder of the Seapoint Center for Collaborative Leadership and co-author of *Full-Steam Ahead! Unleash the Power of Vision in Your Work and Your Life.*

Julia Storberg-Walker: Professor at George Washington University in the Department of Human and Organizational Learning.

Rob Walker: Freelance journalist and author of *The Art of Noticing: 131 Ways to Spark Creativity, Find Inspiration, and Discover Joy in the Everyday.*

Tracie Ward: President and Founder of Celebrations of Life Services and LivingWisely.

Sinikka Waugh: Owner and Founder of Your Clear Next Step.

John Weiss: Artist and author of *An Artful Life: Inspirational Stories and Essays for the Artist in Everyone.*

Breadcrumbs for Further Thought

Since I want this book to have a long shelf life as a resource for years to come, I am sharing some of my top breadcrumbs in each category. These topics will always be relevant and meaningful, which means that the "research" never stops—by being open to breadcrumbs in the world around me, it's difficult to stop noticing them!

So, here is a collection of some of my favorites. This is another way that I am leaving my Breadcrumb Legacy ... a trail you may follow and see where it leads you.

Books

Man's Search for Meaning (Viktor Frankl)

The Power of Regret: How Looking Backward Moves Us Forward (Daniel Pink)

The Second Mountain: The Quest for a Moral Life (David Brooks)

Atomic Habits: An Easy & Proven Way to Build Good Habits & Break Bad Ones (James Clear)

Wisdom@Work: The Making of a Modern Elder (Chip Conley)

The Artist's Way: A Spiritual Path to a Higher Creativity (Julia Cameron)

Claiming Your Place at the Fire: Living the Second Half of Your Life on Purpose (Richard Leider and David Shapiro)

Designing Your Life: How to Build a Well-Lived Joyful Life (Bill Burnett and Dave Evans)

Finding Your Why: A Practical Guide for Discovering Purpose for You and Your Team (Simon Sinek)

How Will You Measure Your Life? (Clayton Christensen, James Allworth, and Karen Dillon)

When All You've Ever Wanted Isn't Enough: The Search for a Life that Matters (Harold Kushner)

The Velveteen Rabbit (Margery Williams)

Designing the Life You Love: A Step-by Step Guide to Building a Mean-
ingful Future (Ayse Birsel)
The Boy, the Mole, the Fox, and the Horse (Charlie Mackesy)
The New Earth: Awakening to Your Life's Purpose (Eckhart Tolle)
The Art of Noticing: 131 Ways to Spark Creativity, Find Inspiration, and
Discover Joy in the Everyday (Rob Walker)
The Man Who Planted Trees (Jean Giono)
The Prophet (Kahlil Gibran)

Poems & Poetry Collections

There Is No Road: Proverbs by Antonio Machado (Antonio Machado;
D. Maloney and M. Berg, Trans.)
"I'm Nobody! Who are you?" (Emily Dickinson, in *The Poems of Emily
Dickinson*, Ed. R.W. Fanklin)
"The Dash" (Linda Ellis)
"Threads" (Jim Autry, in *Love and Profit: The Art of Caring Leadership*)
"It Takes Courage" (Shelly L. Francis, in *The Courage Way: Leading and
Living with Integrity*)
"The Arrow and the Song" (Henry Wadsworth Longfellow, in *The Belfry
of Bruges and Other Poems*)
"Small Kindnesses" (Danusha Laméris)
"Wild Geese", "When Death Comes", "Don't Hesitate" (note the last
line!), "The Summer Day", "The Uses of Sorrow", and "Invitation",
in addition to the collection *Swan: Poems and Prose Poems* (Mary Oliver)

Films

Harold and Maude (Hal Ashby)
Slumdog Millionaire (Danny Boyle)
Paris Is Burning (Jennie Livingston)
Young@Heart (Stephen Walker)
About Schmidt (Alexander Payne)
Everybody's Fine (Kirk Jones)
The Best Exotic Marigold Hotel (John Madden)
The Company Men (John Wells)
Tuesdays with Morrie (Mick Jackson)
The Wizard of Oz (Victor Fleming)
The Karate Kid (John G. Avildsen)
Finding Forrester (Gus Van Sant)
Mrs. Palfrey at the Claremont (Dan Ireland)
Get Low (Robert Duvall)
Up (Pete Docter)

Evening (Lajos Koltai)
The Straight Story (David Lynch)
Mad Hot Ballroom (Marilyn Agrelo)
First Cow (Kelly Reichardt)
Dick Johnson Is Dead (Kirsten Johnson)
The Farewell (Lulu Wang)
Cocoon (Ron Howard)
The Intern (Nancy Meyers)
Peaceful Warrior (Victor Salva)
Inside Out (Pete Docter)
Regarding Henry (Mike Nichols)
They Way (Emilio Estevez)
On Golden Pond (Mark Rydell)

Web Wisdom (Newsletters and Websites)

"On Being" with Krista Tippett
"The Marginalian" by Maria Popova
"The Saturday Newsletter" by John P. Weiss
"Human Values in Aging Newsletter" by Harry "Rick" Moody
"The Sunday Paper" by Maria Shriver
"Wisdom Well" by Chip Conley
"Next Avenue" from Twin Cities PBS
"Friday Forward" by Robert Glazer
"The Art of Noticing" by Rob Walker
Grateful Living (grateful.org)
"Reboot" by Jerry Colonna

Songs

"Humble and Kind" by Tim McGraw
"Live Like You Were Dying" by Tim McGraw
"Lean In" by Little Big Town
"The Life You Chose" by Jason Isbell
"Awake My Soul" by Mumford and Sons
"Present Tense" by Pearl Jam
"Small Things" by Andy Gullahorn
"Rainbow Connection" by Paul Williams and Kenneth Ascher
"Season of Love" by Jonathan Larson

Index